BELLWOOD COWBOY

The Artie Quinton Story

Ted L. Pittman

AuthorHouse™
1663 Liberty Drive
Bloomington, IN 47403
www.authorhouse.com
Phone: 1-800-839-8640

First published by AuthorHouse 1/5/2011

ISBN: 978-1-4520-9681-0 (sc)
ISBN: 978-1-4520-9680-3 (hc)
ISBN: 978-1-4520-9682-7 (e)

Library of Congress Control Number: 2010918311

Printed in the United States of America

This book is printed on acid-free paper.

PROLOGUE

I am deeply honored to be asked to write the life story of Artie Quinton! As I began to work on his biography, the magnitude of this man's influence, not only around the Mill Creek area, but across the state, and across a wide range of demographics was staggering to me. While traveling across the country to interview people who had associations with Artie over the years, I was constantly surprised at the input I received from folks along the way. Almost everyone in this part of the country knows Artie Quinton, and the ones who don't have heard something about him and were ready to share what they knew with me. Artie has touched so many lives in a positive manner over almost a century of living.

While gathering information for this book, I had the opportunity to visit many hours with Artie over a period of several weeks and months. I will always cherish those times with him. As I got to know him better and he shared his remembrances with me, it became more and more apparent to me how remarkable a person he truly is. I was constantly amazed at the level and depth of his mind at the age of ninety-seven years. His memory, even back to a very early age, is excellent and his ability to recall even the smallest detail is fascinating to me. I captured our visits on a little digital recorder and used the material as the outline for this book. I wish I could have captured his expressions as he re-lived the memorable events in his life. The joyous times like walking to church with the love of his life as they got acquainted when she was only sixteen years old. The birth of his daughter Janet, and the times he spent with her as she grew. The sad times like deaths in the family, and the light that would come to his face when he talked about his relationship with God.

Artie grew up in a difficult period in our history as did a few others still living in the area today. His start in life was about as humble as it gets, born in a log cabin in the country north of Mill Creek Oklahoma, and then to lose his birth mother at the age of 17 months. Raised by a loving grandmother and stern but loving grandfather, he managed to keep a positive outlook on life. When, at the age of 12, he lost his grandmother, the only mother he ever knew, it seemed life was just going to keep on dealing him about as rough a hand as you can get.

As a teenager and young man during the Great Depression, Artie experienced firsthand the hardships of the times. Now-a-days, looking back on those times, he believes the Lord had his hand on him through it all. He told me in one of our talks, "The Lord never makes a mistake."

Artie is a veteran and served in the Army from 1934 until

1937 at Ft. Sill near Lawton Oklahoma. He has fond memories of his days in the military even though they kept him away from his sweetheart Agnes McClure.

Artie is a man of impeccable integrity and strength of character. His devotion to his faith is beyond reproach. I recall a statement Darrel Payne made as we visited one night while I was working on the book. ***"Surely, if there is a modern day saint, that saint is Artie Quinton."*** Artie always said, "The Lord didn't call me to preach, but he did give me the gift of gab and I mean to use it as long as I can."

During the many hours, days, and months that I worked on my Historical Fiction "Son Of The Red Earth", I learned a lot about the Great Depression and the hardships associated with living during that period in our history, but my 'one on one' talks with Artie and others in this area gave me a firsthand account that I hadn't had previously. As newlyweds living in a little house with no insulation, no electricity or running water, not even wallpaper on the walls. Working twelve to fourteen hours a day seven days a week with not a day off for five months. This was the life of Artie and his young bride in 1937. How those times must have helped to forge a partnership that would endure for over 63 years of marriage.

I've included a little bit of history of the Bellwood Community throughout the book. This is the area that has been home for Artie most of his life. I've attempted to give readers a feel of how the area looked in the early 1900s, the people who lived in the area, and how they went about their daily lives. By necessity, it was a different way of living when Artie was born and as he grew up in the rural area north of Mill Creek. The hardships were just a part of living in the times and people dealt with them just like they have done for generations. Each generation adds to the rich history of this area and builds on what has gone before.

I've also attempted to include a little humor and storytelling to go along with the history of Artie's life. Cowboy life in itself is a colorful life and has a long enduring history in this part of the country. Artie lived the life of a cowboy for many years and has a satisfied feeling about how he has lived and what his life represents. He has been a stockman and ranch manager with a reputation for knowing cattle and horses and how best to handle them for several decades.

It has been a lot of fun working with Artie and the many others over the past several months. I hope this book gives readers a fresh insight into the man we know as Artie Quinton today. He is truly a special person. I hope you enjoy reading about his life.

ACKNOWLEDGEMENTS AND CONTRIBUTIONS

Janet Quinton Crenshaw for the wealth of information she provided and her faith in me to accomplish this work.

My wife Darlene for the beautiful photography and the cover designs. For the many hours of proofing and for keeping me on track.

The following people contributed to this book either by giving of their time, their stories, or both.

Clyde Runyan

Billye Bob Crenshaw

Doc Easley

Horace and Hazel Cook

Billy Pittman

Don Payne

Kenneth Cole

Frank and Lil Trent

Darrel Payne

Peggy Hood

Gene Lafitte

Tony and Deanna Gordon

Jon Smith

Dr. Turrentine

Brian Tolbert

Harmon Clark

Jerry & Linda George

Mike & Sharline Pitmon

Sam Daube

Janet Quinton Crenshaw

Arvella Northrip

Jim & Vickie Crenshaw

Mr. & Mrs. JE Quinton

Mr. & Mrs. Bobby Howard

Gale Ellis

Bryan Gordon

Ty Crenshaw

Betty Clark

Aileen Holder

Denzil Jordan

Travis Vaughan

Kelly Conner

Larry Hobbs

Brother Eddie Malphrus

Bob & Patsy Hook

Sharon Beratto

Cheryl Parker

Darlene Pittman

Doc Swartz

Dan Howard

Darryl Patrick

DISCLAIMER

The depiction of the Bellwood and Mill Creek areas in the early 1900s reflected in this book is a compilation of the memories of folks living today and records that might have been available for reference. The location of homes and businesses and the people who lived and worked there may not be completely correct for the times, but is how folks remembered it to be. Spelling of names may not be correct in all instances. Stories in the book are as told by various friends, relatives, and acquaintances of people who were involved and the integrity of the stories is only as good as the memories of the storytellers. Birth dates and event dates are thought to be correct in all instances, but are also subject to memory in some cases.

DEDICATION

This work is dedicated to Artie Otto Quinton and Agnes McClure Quinton. They are true pioneers in their own right. They did it the right way and will reap their rewards in Heaven.

CONTENTS

INTRODUCTION
A STORY FROM BELLWOOD'S EARLY DAYS

The Bellwood community was wild and wooly back in the mid to late 1800s as was most of the state of Oklahoma. It was not a place for the faint of heart and if there was any law, it was too little and too far away to be of much good when needed. Most everyone went armed and for good reason. The following story is an example of what could and did happen.

A couple of men from the sparsely populated Bellwood area decided to spend a few days fishing on the Washita River. For the purposes of this story, we'll call them Bud and Fred. It took them all day to make the ride to the river and it was getting on late in the afternoon when they arrived at the selected fishing spot. They found a perfect spot in the bend of the river where the water had gouged out a deep hole just right for catfish. As they made their way down to the water, they came upon something totally unexpected, a fresh grave just up a ways from the edge of the river bank. It put the scare into them for a minute, but then they thought, "what the heck," whoever was buried in that grave wasn't gonna hurt them any.

They moved off down the river a little way and set up camp. They had just gotten their lines in the water when they heard a noise behind them. Turning, they saw a man and a woman sitting on their horses and they were both pointing guns right at them.

"Who are you and what are you doing here?" the woman asked.

"We're just a couple of guys looking to maybe catch a few catfish," Bud replied. "How come you got them guns pointed at us? We ain't done nothing."

"What do you boys know about the man in that there fresh grave?" The woman asked.

"We don't know nothing," Fred answered. "We just got here a few minutes ago ourselves. Ain't been here long enough to get a camp set up proper, hardly."

"You boys sure you didn't run onto that guy and help him into that grave?" The man asked. "Yawl look awful suspicious to me. Let me introduce the lady to you gents. This here is Belle Starr, and I'm her right hand man, you might say. We've got a man missing and we suspect he's in that grave up there on the riverbank. We don't know for sure if it is him or how he might have got into that fix, but you guys are here and they ain't nobody else around, so far as I'm concerned, you're the guilty parties."

"Tell you what we're gonna do," Belle said. "It's too late this evening, but come morning, you two gents are gonna dig up that body up there and if it is our man and he has a bullet hole in him, you boys are dead meat."

Bud and Fred looked at each other. "What if he ain't got a bullet hole in him? Bud asked. "What's gonna happen to us?"

"I ain't decided about that," Belle replied. "You boys just better hope there ain't no bullet hole in that man is all I got to say."

Well now, it's safe to say that Bud and Fred didn't get much sleep that night. Neither did Belle Starr and her hired henchman for that matter. The year was 1876 and Belle had been recently widowed. Her reign as an outlaw was in its infancy. If she was going to gain and keep the respect of a bunch of outlaws, she was going to have to avenge the death of one of her men. It was looking for all the world like Bud and Fred were gonna pay that price.

The sun came up over the trees to the east of the camp just like it did every morning. The deer that came down to the river to drink just after sun-up were oblivious to the drama that was playing out just up the river in the camp of the four humans. For Bud and Fred, life was standing still. Did they have but a matter of an hour or so to live? Would they ever see another sunrise? These and other thoughts were running through their minds as they made their way up the hill to the grave with Belle following close behind with her gun pointed right at their backs. Fred was wondering if their bodies would ever be found. Would his wife ever know what happened to him? Bud, on the other hand, was trying to figure a way out of this mess. He had made up his mind that if the body was Belle's man, and he had a bullet hole in him, he was not going down without a fight. He had his pocket knife right there in his left front pocket where he always carried it, and while it was no match for a forty five, it at least gave him a fighting chance if it came down to that.

Though the grave was shallow, it took them over an hour to reach the body with the little camp shovel Belle pilfered from Fred's gear. When the man's plaid shirt came into view, Belle looked over into the grave.

"Pull him out of there," she said. "Roll him over the side of the grave and then step back." I want a good look at him before you climb out of that grave, There might not be any need for you to crawl out of there anyway. Might just save me the trouble of rolling you back in there."

Fred took the corpse by the shoulders and with Bud handling the other end, they managed to roll him up and out of the grave onto the grass beside it. They stepped back against the far side of the grave and stood there waiting for Belle to inspect the body.

"It's John alright, "she said. "I don't see a bullet hole in him though. Looks to me like he might have drowned. Ride up the river a ways Charlie, and see if you see any sign of his horse, she said. The man she called Charlie mounted his horse and was soon out of sight over a little rise to the east.

"Looks like this proves we didn't kill this man," Bud said. "I'd say he drowned trying to cross the river. Lots of fellars can't swim you know."

"If that's what happened, who do you suppose buried him?"

Belle wanted to know. "He didn't dig that grave and then crawl into it and cover his self up, that's for sure. Besides, I haven't made up my mind what to do with you two galoots." Just then, they heard the sound of horses coming down the river at a gallop. It was Charlie and he was leading a saddled horse.

"Found him about a half mile up the river," he said. "It's John's horse sure enough. Ain't no blood on the saddle or nothing, but I can tell this saddle has been wet not long ago."

"That proves he drowned then," Bud allowed. "We told you we didn't know nothing about it. What say you let us go now?"

"I'm a good mind to just shoot you to shut you up," Belle said. "I've heard about all I want to hear from the two of you. You get out of that there grave and roll John back into it. When you get him covered back up, you're free to go. That is if you keep your mouths shut while you're doing it."

Fred and Bud wasted no time getting John properly buried again. In no time at all they were packed and ready to leave. Belle and Charlie sat their horses and watched them go.

"Ain't nobody gonna believe this when we tell 'em," Bud said. "I wouldn't believe it myself if I hadn't been here." Fred gave him a knowing look.

By the time Artie was born in 1912, this area of the state was a little more civilized. Almost nobody carried a gun, at least in plain sight, and the days of the Belle Starr Gang were but a memory of the past. Times were still hard, and would become even harder if possible with the Great Depression looming just around the corner. Such is the history of the area. The country was fast becoming more settled in and around the Bellwood

Community. The history of one of the greatest men in this part of the country was about to begin. Artie Quinton helped shape the country and the people around this area of Oklahoma for the next century. What a legacy he will leave. What a man he has been!

PART 1:
DAY ONE OF A CENTURY

It is a common sight to see Artie Quinton walking along the streets of Mill Creek, Oklahoma clad in his blue coveralls and pushing his walker ahead of him. Folks know to watch for his slight figure as he plods steadily along. Artie has been walking these streets a long time, first about five miles per day for many years, then three miles, and now, the last several months, about a mile and a half. Not bad for his almost ninety-eight years. Artie lives alone these days, in a little white house just east of the Holiness Church he has attended since the early 1940s. He didn't plan it this way, but God has a way of changing your plans when you least expect it.

Things have sort of been this way since his loving wife Ag went to be with the Lord on July 25th 2000. It's not easy living alone, especially with the handicap of being legally blind, but you never hear him complain. Artie walks to church every day to pray, been doing it for a long time. He has a lot of friends drop by to visit and his ready smile is your welcome when you ring his door bell.

I know one of these days; I won't be able to see Artie in his favorite seat at the end of the pew, half way down the row of pews on the south side of the church sanctuary. Each Sunday, as I make my way into the church, my eyes search him out to make sure he is there. I will miss his greeting, "Hello Cuz, how you doing" and his hand on my shoulder. His presence gives me a feeling of security, as if his being there ensures that all is well with our little church and things are as they should be. I ask him how he's doing and the answer is always the same. "I'm just a doin", he says.

Let's start with a picture of Artie in his familiar blue coveralls and orange vest pushing the walker along the street as he makes his daily round. Then let's begin to re-wind his life back through the years, the happy times in the little house where he still lives, years on the West Ranch with Ag, back to the birth of his daughter Janet, the hardships and adventures of running the feed lot in the 1930s, courtship and marriage, the years spent in service to his country, the school years at Bellwood, all the way back to the little rented log cabin about four miles north of Mill Creek on the Sallie Gaddis allotment where it all started almost a century ago. A house where Robert Pierce Quinton and his young wife Bessie Howard Quinton were carving out a life in the country on the west side of the Bellwood Community. They had been married only a short time, but long enough to conceive the baby boy that would be born ten and a half months into the young marriage. Artie's uncle Albert "Ab" Howard told him a few years later, that they had been out working in the fields and when they came in for lunch, there he was. He was born after breakfast and was waiting for them when they came in at noon to eat. There had been some controversy over the exact location of Artie's birthplace until several sources that were actually there cleared up any misconception several years later.

Left---- Artie's mother Bessie Howard Quinton
Right--- Artie with his papa Pierce Quinton shortly after his mother died

Artie would live in that house from the time his mother died until he was six years old, and they would prove to be tumultuous years for him. At the very young age of seventeen months, he lost his mother to death during a difficult childbirth. It was a time in the history of the area where medical services were very limited. Pain management was almost unheard of at the time and when it became apparent that a cesarean birth was the only thing left to try, she just was not strong enough to handle the ordeal. Cesarean birth was not common at that time, and the knowledge to do it correctly was not there that night. Sadly, the result was the death of both Artie's mother and the baby.

Bessie Howard Quinton was born in Texas on October 2, 1892 and died March 24, 1914. She was twenty-one and a half years old at her death. It was a turning point in Artie's young life. What is a child, barely a toddler, to do without a mother, and with a father that had to work to make a living for what was left of his family? At the cemetery, Artie's maternal grandmother and grandfather, Martha and Ben Howard, asked his father if they could adopt him. He said they couldn't adopt him, but they could raise him as their own. A few years later, Artie asked his dad why his dad's parent didn't raise him since they were both still living at the time. His dad told him that he let his Grandma Martha raise him because she was the best Christian woman he knew.

Top row left to right. Cecil Howard, William Albert (Ab) Howard, Edwin Howard, Ben Howard.
Bottom row left to right. Etta Howard, Leonard Howard, Artie Quinton, Martha Howard. Picture was taken the summer of 1914 after Artie's mother Bessie Howard Quinton died in March.

(Author's Note :)
The words to this poem came to me as I was writing one day. I had a Howard family picture in front of me and as I reflected on it, the words started to flow. I hope readers can see Artie's life in the verses.

I SEE A CHILD

I see a child with skin so fair
With rosy cheeks and snow white hair.
I see him in his little bed
The pillow where he lays his head

He has no ma to hold him tight
To kiss his cheek and say good night
She left him there, she had no choice
One day with her, he will rejoice.

So he must be, a little man
And he will do, the best he can.
To hold her memory in his mind
With body strong and spirit kind.

I see him as he walks to school
To learn to read the golden rule.
So he can be, a boy that she
Would be proud of, if she could see.

I see him as a strong young man
With handsome face and skin so tan
Where is the child of yesterday?
Who worked so hard and seldom played.

Who is the girl she is so fair
With rosy cheeks and golden hair.
He walks with her and holds her hand
On life's short road with her he'll stand

Their love is deep it's meant to last
The future grows out of the past
Together now with no refrain
Forever so they will remain

He holds the child she gave to him
His love for her will never dim
Life now is full as life can be
Add one more branch now to the tree

Oh love so pure where have you gone
He sits alone now on the throne
For she is gone for just awhile
He'll see her soon and her sweet smile.

Alone once more why is it so.
Why must it be he wants to know
He'll hold her memory in his mind
With body strong and spirit kind

'Til once again he'll hold her hand
As they stroll 'cross the promised land
The mothers there that had no choice
The tears flow now as they rejoice.

The light shines bright down from the throne
He sees his Savior there alone.
He reaches out and takes the hand
And steps into, the promised land.

Ted L. Pittman

THE HOWARD FAMILY

Before we move on, let's take this opportunity to talk about the family and the setting that would be home to Artie for the next several years of his life. Ben and Martha Howard had several children of their own at the time Artie went to live with them. They were his aunts and uncles, but he always thought of them as his brothers and sisters since he grew up as part of the family. The following is a breakdown of the Howard family that was such a big part of Artie's life.

Edwin Howard. (Edwin was about 19 years old when Artie started living with the Howards. He was born in Texas in 1895 and would die in 1918 of the influenza. The flu was especially bad in the winter of 1918 and claimed many lives, especially among the rural communities where medical services were scant at best and non-existent in many cases.)

Etta Howard. (Etta was 15 years old when Artie's mother died. She was born December 31, 1898, also in Texas, and lived until the ripe old age of ninety five. Etta married Turner Pittman and they raised five children, three girls and two boys. The girls were named Edna, Bernice, and Jean, and the twin boys were Boyd and Floyd. They also lost three children, Parthey, Elsie, and Buddy. Etta was 15 years old at the time Artie moved in with the Howards.)

William Albert. ("Ab" Howard was 13 years old when Artie joined the family. He was born April 8th, 1901 and died February 12th, 1973. Ab first married Flora Holder and they had a daughter they named Letha. His second wife was Cozette Beesly and they had a son they named Bobby Gene. Ab later married Jeanette Goshameyer.) He was a colorful character and was prone to partake of the spirits a little too much on occasion. He rode the rails and roamed the country and was pretty much a free spirit for much of his life. In later years, Ab was at Leonard and Edith's house one day and Leonard's son Bobby noticed Ab writing on a piece of paper as he sat at the kitchen table.

"What you doing Uncle Ab," he said.

"Why, I'm writing a letter to myself," Ab replied.

"What does it say?" Bobby wanted to know.

"Don't rightly know," Ab replied. "I won't get it for three or four days." Ab was about thirteen years old when Artie's mother passed away.

Cecil Howard. (Cecil had just turned 11 years old when Arties mother died. He was born March 14th, 1903 and died September 20th 1993. He married Geneva Burk and together they had three children, Benny, Jerry, and Shirley Kaye.)

Leonard Howard. (Leonard was almost 6 years old when

Artie became a part of the family. He was born June 23rd, 1908 and died January 2nd, 1983. He married Edith Miller and they had two sons, Billy and Bobby. He was four years old when Artie became a part of the family.)

Raymond Howard. (Raymond was born a little over a year after Artie's mother died. He was born April 6th, 1915 and died May 19th, 2003. Artie was two and a half years old and already living with the Howards when Raymond was born. Raymond married Edith Spears and they had three sons, Eddie Frank, Danny, and David.)

Emma Howard. (Emma was the baby of the family. She was born March 4th, 1917 and died November 8th, 2004. She was married to Frank Gaines. They had an infant son that was born and died on Christmas Day 1935. Artie was home on leave from the Army at the time. They also had a daughter named Peggy Joyce. Artie was almost four and a half years old when Emma was born.)

Most folks around the area were poor people in terms of finances when Artie was just a little tyke. The kids would go barefoot all summer and would usually get a new pair of shoes before cold weather set in. You had better take good care of those shoes because they had to last until it got warm enough to go barefoot again the next spring. One fall when Artie was about six years old, he got a new pair of shoes. He was so proud of those shoes; he wanted to sleep with them. Folks would wear blue jeans until the knees got holes in them, then they would put a patch on and keep wearing them. When the patch wore out, they'd put another patch over the old patch if the jeans looked like they might hold together a little while longer. It paid to be conservative.

The Howards were good people and Martha Howard was the only mother Artie ever knew. He was just too young to have any memory of his biological mother. His grandma's name was Martha Adeline. Most folks called her Martha, but Ben called her Addie. Artie called her Mother. In the ten plus years he lived with her before her death, he never heard her raise her voice or heard her say a bad word about anybody. One of Artie's earliest memories of her is of her praying. Martha Howard's maiden name was Anderson and she was raised in Texas. When Emma Howard was just a little tyke, Martha took Leonard, Raymond, Emma, and Artie to Texas to see her mother, the children's grandmother. She was Artie's great grandmother. They went on the train as did most folks in those days if they had very far to go. They stayed a couple of days and then stopped and visited with Martha's sister on the way home. It was the only time Artie ever saw either one of them.

Ben Howard was a hard worker and expected the same from his children, including Artie. Artie learned at a young age, when Ben told you to do something, you did it. Wasn't no back talking or hum-hawing around, you just did it. You never heard Ben Howard use foul language, but he had a by-word he used religiously." J***ohn Brown***", he'd say when something wasn't going to suit him. He wouldn't get many sentences out of his mouth 'til here would come another "***John Brown***". He had a voice that carried like a trumpet. If he needed to get your attention and you happened to be thirty or forty feet away from him, he would holler loud enough for folks a couple of hundred yards away to hear what he said. He didn't dole out a lot of corporal punishment, but on at least one occasion, when Artie and Raymond were having a cotton boll fight, just throwing them at each other like boys will do, Ben hollered for them to quit. As boys will do, Artie had to throw another couple of bolls before he quit. He happened to run close enough to Ben for Ben to grab him as he went by, and he got a pretty good swatting with a switch Ben had close to hand. It scared him more than it hurt him, but it served to reinforce the fact that when Ben Howard told you to do something, you might better be doing it.

The house in Bellwood Community where Artie spent most of the formative years of his life was like most every other house in the area at the time. No electricity, of course, and no running water. There was a pump on the well outside where the water bucket for the house was filled and the water for the livestock was pumped on a daily basis. Water for cooking had to be pumped and brought into the house as well. There was an outhouse out back, and it was hotter than the outside temperature in the summer and at least as cold as the outside temperature in the winter. Didn't take too long to do your business when it was twenty degrees outside, that's for sure.

The house had two wood stoves, one in the living room for heat and the cook stove in the kitchen. Ben Howard would usually be the first one up and would get the fire going in the stove in the living room in the wintertime. There would usually be a few coals left from the big log that was banked up at bed time the night before. He would take some coals and get the fire started in the cook stove in the kitchen as well.

One of the first chores Artie had was to pump water for the hogs they kept. It was an everyday job. Raymond was too short to reach the pump handle, so when it came his turn to pump, he would stand on a wooden box so he could reach the pump handle. Everybody had work to do.

They really didn't have much overhead. The only thing they bought at the store besides the bare necessities of groceries was kerosene. Kerosene was used only when necessary for the lamps. It was a necessity to be conservative.

Top row left to right. (Bessie Howard, Artie's mother), Etta Howard, Martha Howard, Edwin Howard, (Letitia Howard, Ben's mother) Ben Howard.
Bottom Row left to right. Cecil Howard, Ab Howard, (Leonard Howard standing on stool) This picture was taken before Artie was born, probably in late 1910 or early 1911.

At the time, there was only one car in the Bellwood Community and it belonged to Ben Howard's brother Burn. Most everybody had a wagon and team, and if you went anywhere, that's how you went. That or maybe on horseback. The only other alternative was 'shank's mare.' The Bellwood Community, in those days, was a thriving rural community of about forty farms and houses. A listing of most of the homes and residents are included in a later chapter.

Mr. Wells moved into the Bellwood area in the early 1920s and he brought with him some fine steel-dust horses. He had a two-seated hack that he would drive around and put on a fine show. Henry Pittman never owned a car until he traded a mule to Bob Goodson for an old Model "T". There was a lot of trading that took place in those days.

In 1922, J.W. Bray ran for County Commissioner of District #3. For a lot of years, Freddy Chapman ruled District #3 and he talked J.W. into running. At that time, the Commissioner terms were four year terms. Jake Trammel was selling out and moving to west Texas at the time, and J.W. told him he sure wished he would stay until after the election. He thought he might need the vote and he knew Jake would vote for him if he was here.

To be a County Commissioner, a man needed to know how to drive. J.W. bought an old car but he didn't have a clue how to drive the thing. At the time, he was assigned as guardian over the Kemp Estate, and one of the Kemp girls, Frankie was her name, taught him how to drive. They had a circle about a quarter of a mile in circumference worn out in the pasture where J.W. would just go around and around trying to get the feel of the thing. He'd start and stop and practice turning until he finally got it down well enough to get out on the road. He drove that car until 1925 and then he bought a brand new 1925 Chevrolet. He drove that Chevy everywhere, even to the cotton patch. Artie figured he must really be up town if he could afford to drive a brand new car to the cotton patch.

Mrs. McDonald came into the Bellwood area when Artie was just a little boy. She had eight children. Her latest husband had passed away over at Hobart, Oklahoma some time back. It was rumored she had been married seven times. She and the kids had all spent some time in Washington State picking apples. John and Ott McDonald were teenage boys at the time and both of them had girlfriends. The girls were sisters and would be the first two of three Quinton sisters that married McDonald brothers. You would see John and Ott coming across the country on horseback and riding like a couple of wild Indians. John and Ruby married first then Ott married his girlfriend "Kid". They drove all the way to Sulphur in a wagon to get married and it was cold as all get out. Ott was 21 years old and Kid was 13 when they got married. Kid always said that there could be nobody any better to anyone than Mrs. McDonald was to her. Still, being married at 13 years of age, in those times couldn't have been too much of a bargain. Of course, at that time, a lot of girls married at 14 or 15 years old.

Artie started to school at Bellwood in 1918 at the age of six. His first teacher was Ozzie Hyden. It was a mile and a half walk to school from the Howard place. Artie would often spend a full week with Earnest and Lizzie Calloway who lived much closer to the school. Lizzie was his Grandpa's sister and she really took a shine to Artie. He would walk to school on Monday morning, then when school let out for the day, he would walk to Earnest and Lizzies. Then when school let out on Friday afternoon, he would walk back home to the Howards for the weekend.

THE LITTLE BOY

The trail wound down through the woods to the bend on Polecat Creek where the log crossing stood white in the morning light. The cedar trees, with their snow covered boughs, were almost ghostly in appearance as they stood their silent vigil alongside the path. The wind was very cold and the little boy drew his jacket closer about his neck as he struggled through the drifts. He was almost there; just over the log that served as a footbridge across Polecat Creek, then up the hill the rest of the way to the school house sitting lonely in the field of white snow. It was not easy for a six year old boy, the mile and a half walk to school that winter of 1918. But then, nothing had ever been easy for him. He never knew his mother; she died when he was just short of seventeen months old. He didn't know it as he walked that day, but he would lose a second mother, the grandmother who was raising him, just six short years later. His toes inside the brogan shoes felt like they were frozen solid as he eased across the snow covered log that lay across the creek. As he made his way up the hill to the school house, snow began to fall again. Soon though, he would be huddled by the wood stove with a chance to thaw out his little frozen hands and feet. He would walk the short distance to Earnest and Lizzie's house after school rather than face the long walk home through the snow.

After Mr. Hyden left, Allen Mathis took over the teaching duties. The only other teacher that taught during Artie's school days was Otherine Standifer Kingsberry. She was married to Jude Kingsberry and gave the students the option of calling her Mrs. Kingsberry or Miss Otherine. They decided they would call her Miss Otherine. One day Miss Otherine took the kids squirrel hunting during school. Somebody asked Jude if she took a squirrel dog. He said "Naw, she didn't need a squirrel dog. Them boys could spot every squirrel in the country and climb every tree there was."

There were, of course, no bathrooms at the school, so everyone used the outhouse. There were about forty kids in school at Bellwood most of the time in those days. There were three Quinton girls in school with Artie at that time. Helen was born in 1911 and was a year older than Artie. Ellen was born in 1914 and Leota, they called her "Red Head," was a 1916 model. ***(Author's note: These three girls were my mother's sisters.)***

There was a community water bucket that all the kids drank from using the same dipper. That was common in those days. Usually, if one kid came down with something, they all caught it before it ran its course. They would take turns going to the well to fill the bucket with water. Sometimes, a grasshopper or some other insect would fly into the filled bucket on the way back to the schoolhouse. No problem, just pick the thing out of the water and go on.

Earnest and Lizzie had a boy named Earl, and he would get up early in the morning during the cold months and go down to the school to get a fire started. By the time school took up for the day, it would be about as warm as it was going to get in the schoolhouse. For this service, Earl earned twenty-five cents per day.

In the 1930's Mrs. Garrison, cooked at the school for a number of years. She was the mother of Hazel Garrison Cook, and Artie's best friend, Elmore Garrison mentioned elsewhere in this book. The last year school was held at Bellwood was school year 1943 and 1944. The teacher was a lady named Pansy Kate Conley and Bonnie Pitmon was a first grader that year.

There were several rural schools in the area at that time. Frisco, which was west of the Bellwood District, Pilgrims Rest, Browns Valley over by Spring Creek, (sometimes Jack McClure was the only student there), Fletcher, Al Hambra School, and the Fred Hunt School. There were also schools at Reagan, Troy, Concrete, and Mill Creek. Pilgrims Rest was the first school to consolidate with the Mill Creek School District. Three school districts met and cornered on the Daube Ranch at the time, Frisco, Bellwood, and Mill Creek.

On occasion, Artie would stay a few days with his papa. Pierce worked for Daube's at the time and while he was working, Mrs. West would watch Artie. George West was foreman at the time and he had a stepson who attended school as well. One day Artie witnessed an incident that never left his memory. George West's stepson was riding his little bay horse "Charlie" to school and was racing him pretty fast down by Burn Howard's place. When George found out about it, he whipped him with a buggy whip. It was shocking to Artie and he never did believe it was justified. Horse racing was common at the time and a lot of folks rode pretty fast on occasion. He never forgot that episode, however. George died with the flu in 1918, the same year Edwin Howard died of the same cause. They were in the same room while they were sick and folks would come and sit up with them.

There was an old man living around there at the time who was an old oil field worker. His name was Hugh Crump, but everybody called him "Muleskinner." For some unknown reason, he called George West "Mrs. Mitchell." There was undoubtedly an inside joke there somewhere but nobody ever figured out what it was.

Turner Pittman was sitting up with the sick folks one night and Muleskinner happened by to check on them. He looked them over good and then in his distinct Oklahoma brogue, declared as how somebody better see to Mrs. Mitchell, he was about to "kick the bucket." Sure enough, he died and is buried in the Mill Creek Cemetery.

Artie attended school at Bellwood through the eighth grade. There was no high school at Bellwood and he never got the opportunity to attend high school.

BELLWOOD SCHOOL DISTRICT

1918-1927

Artie attended Bellwood School from the fall of 1918 until the spring of 1927. The home where he lived with his grandparents, Ben and Martha Howard, was a mile and a half from the school house. The original Bellwood School House was made of logs and was located north of the school house where Artie went to school. It was, of course, a rural school, and all the students lived in the general area and had similar journeys to school. They came on foot, on horseback, in wagons, or however they could get there. George Patrick made a little cart for the Patrick kids to ride to school in. It was pulled by a little horse. They came, for the most part, in good weather and bad.

There were no school buses at the time. When the Mill Creek School first started running school buses, the bus drivers owned the buses and acted sort of like contractors to the school district. Later, the school districts, with help from the State Government, bought buses and hired drivers to drive them. The school was in session for two months during the summer so the kids could be out in the fall to pick cotton and help get the crops in.

The most famous, or should I say ***infamous***, event that happened in all the years the Bellwood School was in operation was the killing of Fillmore English's son between the school and the outhouse one day in or about 1912. The English boy had gone to the outhouse and was returning to the school. Carlos Beasley was headed to the outhouse and had an old pistol with him. It's not clear what happened, but the pistol went off and killed the English boy. The only witness to the incident was Carlos himself and he claimed it was an accident. A lengthy trial took place, but the killing was finally ruled an accident. Carlos Beasley went on to become World Champion Saddle Bronc Rider in 1920. He returned to the Bellwood area on occasion for a few years. He would ride a freight train in and stay a few days, then catch another freight out.

Looking at the Bellwood area today, one would be hard pressed to understand the makeup of the area in the first three or four decades of the 20th century. The district was well populated, and sustained an average school attendance of around forty pupils. I'm going to attempt to paint a picture of how the area looked in those days, where the houses were, and who lived in them at the time. If, as a reader, you are not familiar with the area, it may be difficult to see, in your mind's eye, the layout of the area, but you may recall some of the families that lived there at the time.

I'm going to lay the north boundary point as present day Stinson Road and place the houses from that point. The road turns south just east of Horace and Hazel Cook's place and becomes Bellwood Road. The Bellwood School was well east of the road, about a mile south of the corner. On down the road in the southerly direction there is an "S" curve and Pennington Creek bisects the road at Bray Bridge. For many years, this bridge was known as "The Red Bridge." The houses in the area were as follows.

The main ranch house on East Daube Ranch.

The log house west of the ranch house. Mr. Winchester lived there.

Richard Pitmon lived on the 100 acres Daube's owned east of present day Bellwood road and south of the Bray Bridge.

Alton Bell Pitmon lived in the house just south of the Bray Bridge.

Bray House located north of the bridge. Ethel Lewis lived there. Her husband, "Ovie" was killed in a smelter accident in Henrietta, Oklahoma. She bought the place by the Bray Bridge with the insurance money she received from his accident.

Log rent house on Sallie Gaddis's place where Artie was born. It was located about a half mile west of the Bray Bridge.

Sallie Gaddis's lived on the same allotment as the rent house was on. Liz Gaddis had two houses north and west of Sallie's place.

Dave Bulman lived close to Pennington Creek north of present day Stinson Road.

Turner McKinney had a place west of Pennington Creek and adjacent to present day Stinson Road.

Bill Cook and Horace Cook had houses just north of Stinson Road.

Pete McClure's place was located about a half mile north of the Cooks' houses. Bessie and Bill Cook had a house close to Pete's in the early 1930s.

Artie and Ag moved a house in just south of Horace Cook's place in the early 1940s. They never lived in this house. Arvel and Jo Pitmon lived there for a while and the place was eventually sold to Ott McDonald.

Claude and Mabel Gaddis had houses on the creek and each had 160 acres of land.

Pierce and Nellie Quinton, Artie's dad and stepmother, had two houses, both on the west side of Bellwood Road.

Dorothy Mae Thompson had two houses on the ranch east of the road.

Will Bray had a ten acre orchard north of the Bray Bridge and south of Roy Quinton's place in the 1930s. He had spaced the trees so he could plow both directions. His son Everett would load a dump truck with produce from the orchard and go to Sulphur, Wynnewood, and Paul's Valley selling whatever he had gathered for a dollar a bushel.

Jim Smith lived in a house between Will Bray's place and the Bellwood School House.

There was a house south of the Bellwood School house about half a mile and Jake Garrison lived there for a while. The old chimney still stands today.

The Gaines family lived several different places and had a place west of present day Bellwood Road in the 1930s. They lived on Sallie Gaddis's allotment for a while around 1940.

Nelson Colbert lived on forty acres south of the Bellwood School House.

Roy Quinton lived on a ten acre place at the north end of present day Bellwood Road. Roy married a girl named Pearl and they had two children, a boy named Tommy and a girl they called Dink. Probably was a nickname, and it's not clear what her given name was. Pearl was quite the tomboy while growing up and would squirrel hunt with the boys and generally do about anything the boys would do. Pearl died when her children were still very young.

Turner and Etta Pittman lived in a log house east of the Gaines place on Claude Gaddis's allotment..

Hamp Holt lived in a log house close to the Gaines place.

Watson Carter lived east of the Bellwood School. He had a son named Charlie who was Artie's really good friend. They called him "Sonny Boy".

George Burk lived in a two story log house on the Carter allotment. The Burks lived north of the Bray Bridge and west of Pennington Creek in the 1930s and lost their house to the famous tornado of 1933.

The log house by Polecat Creek where Grandma and Grandpa Burk lived.

Bill Burk house a mile north of Grandma and Grandpa Burk's place.

John Beasley lived half a mile northwest of the Burks' on the Kemp Estate. There were three or four houses on the Kemp estate.

Arvel and Jo Pitmon lived north-east of the school house on the Thompson Ranch. They also lived in Artie and Ag's house west of present day Bellwood Road for a time. Then later in the house adjacent to the main ranch house where Dorothy Thompson lived.

The Ben Howard family moved from the Sallie Gaddis place to a house on the east side of present day Bellwood Road and almost due east of the school house about a mile and a half. The house was east of Pennington Creek. Artie lived there from age six to age twenty.

Jake Trammel had a house on Dry Branch not far from where the Patrick families live today.

Uncle Tom Quinton lived in a little house just east of Jake Trammel's place. There was another house a little farther east of Tom's place.

Walter Seeley lived in the house on the hill a mile west and a half a mile south of Horace Cook's place. ***(Author's note: Walter Seeley's son Ben married my Aunt Viola. I've known her as Aunt Babe all my life.)*** Originally, the Seeleys lived east of the Bellwood School House.

Herschel Trammel lived north of the Seeley place. He was Glenn and Leo Trammel's dad. Tom Clement lived north of present day Stinson Road and about a mile north of the Seeley house.

Rome Slaughter lived where George Patrick's orchard was at one time. "Old Man Slaughter," Rome's dad, lived east of the Walter Seeley place.

The house built at the feed pens in 1937 ends the residences in the Bellwood School District at the time.

I have attempted to place all the houses as best I could from what long- time residents of the area could recall. It must be noted that people moved around quite a lot in those days. Artie and his daughter Janet supplied much of the information. Please forgive any miscalculations or wrong spellings of names. I hope this listing gives readers a general feel of how the Bellwood School District was laid out in the years Artie attended school there and up into the 1930s. The school district was four miles by five mile consisting of twenty square miles. There were at least 48 houses in the school district in 1932.

In the 1930s, the Bellwood School would host many revivals and the precursor of the Mill Creek Pentecostal Holiness Church was formed there. The area has a rich history of cotton farming, cattle ranching, and country living in a time when the state was young and really growing. Times were tough, nobody had any money to speak of, and the Great Depression was right around the corner when Artie first started school at Bellwood. His schooling there gave him the foundation to be successful in life. Like many, he had only an eighth grade education. It was good enough to allow him to be what he wanted to be in life. In many ways, he is the most educated man I know. His knowledge of the Bible is unsurpassed among the people I have known and with whom I have had dealings in my life. Artie is my second cousin; his father Pierce Quinton and my grandfather Will Quinton were brothers. I am proud to call him family.

SHOPPING IN EARLY DAY MILL CREEK

About all the shopping that was done by the Howard family was done in the town of Mill Creek, Oklahoma. It would take about an hour and a half to get to town in the wagon. Artie was twelve years old the first time he went to Sulphur. He went with his Papa and Nellie. Artie's papa Pierce had a 1925 Ford and they went into Sulphur around by Veteran's Lake. When they got to the top of the hill by the Bromide Hill lookout, they stopped the car. Nellie told Artie to look north and he could see Sulphur. It was the first time he had ever seen buildings larger than a two story house.

Those days, you didn't just go to town on a whim. The trip was planned so that everything that needed to be done or bought was taken care of on a single trip. A trip to town was a treat and the family would load up in the wagon and make a day of it. There was a good selection of businesses at Mill Creek, and you could purchase just about anything you were likely to need. There were three blacksmith shops in town and were run by Isaac Dennis, Bob Stalcup, and Uncle Dick Faulkner. Blacksmith shops, in those days, furnished a variety of services from horse shooing to plow sharpening, and could usually make about anything from metal that you couldn't buy anywhere else.

There were two banks operating in the early 1920s to serve the ranchers and farmers of the area. There was a lot of cotton grown in the area and most folks would borrow enough money to put in a cotton crop and then pay the loan off when the crop came in. Wagon yards were the early day version of motels and folks would park the wagons in the wagon yard and sleep in the wagon or on pallets on the ground. Mill Creek had two wagon yards when Artie was a youngster.

Mr. Young moved into Mill Creek in 1918 and put in the first garage. Isaac Sparks ran a produce and took care of the Methodist Church as well. There was another produce shop run by a Mr. Dudley. Mr. Dudley branched out into the fur business and had a spot in the back of the store where you could sell furs of any kind. Opossums, coyotes, and coons were the most common, but he would buy about any kind of fur you would bring in. He bought pecans in the store as well.

Upstairs over the Dudley Produce Shop was the telephone office. Ruth Price was the telephone operator and Leota Quinton worked there as well. Charlie and Ruth Ozment had a telephone office in their living room at one time.

Henry Howell had a combination grocery and hardware

store. Jim Lester and a man by the name of Mr. Brewer ran the two cotton gins that were operating at the time. When the cotton crops started coming in, there would be wagon loads of cotton lined up waiting to unload at the gins. Bennett Grocery was in operation from 1918 when Artie was six years old, until 1929. A man named Purcell purchased the store from Mr. Bennett at the time, but sold it back to Mr. Bennett a short time later. J.T. Clement bought the store from Mr. Bennett at that time and ran it for many years.

Tom Hoosier also ran a grocery and dry goods store. You could buy a Stetson hat for $5.00 in 1930 at Tom Hoosiers Store. Good khaki pants and a shirt for $2.50. One hundred pounds of sugar or beans for $5.00, big cans of red salmon were 25 cents a can and the big candy bars were a nickel. Gasoline was 10 cents a gallon and propane was 8 cents a gallon. You could buy bread that was a couple of days old, three loaves for a quarter.

When Artie was just a little tyke, his uncle Ab Howard would take him to town horseback and they would usually end up at Tom Hoosiers grocery Store. Ab worked for Daubes at the time and had a steady income. He introduced Artie to Tom and told him to let Artie have anything in the store he wanted and to charge it on his account. Artie didn't want to be a burden to Ab so he never took advantage of his generosity. Then one day when he had been in town most of the day, hungry and broke as usual, he bought a couple of candy bars and charged them on Ab's account. It was the only time he ever used the account. Ab was earning $35.00 a month at the time.

Bennie Reynolds had a barber shop and was in competition with Boss Armstrong who had a barber shop that sported three chairs. Orb Bulman and Joe Cobb also cut hair part of the time. Next to Benny Reynolds Barber Shop was Harold Upfold's Dry Cleaning Shop. Doc Newberry ran the drug store on the north corner just west of the main road that ran through town north and south. The Wright Hotel did a good business as did Belcher's store and station. Frank Stie ran a general store just west of the telephone office and later moved down the street just east of Bennie Reynolds barber Shop. Shine Waller had the first service station in Mill Creek. Mill Creek was a thriving business center in those days.

It was common to see folks riding the freight cars as they would come through town. The depression was taking its toll on folks all over the country and whole families were just looking for work or some way to get by. The early freight engines were steam engines and the water man at the Mill Creek depot was a fellow named Swindale. He had a son they called "Wild Onion". When soup lines were formed in the larger cities like Oklahoma City and Dallas, some folks would just gather up the kids and hop a freight to take advantage of the free food. At least, that way, they could make sure the kids were fed. Times were rough. Money was scarce and there were few jobs to be had. If you had a job of any kind, you were one of the more fortunate ones.

Shack villages sprung up around the areas where the soup lines were operating and folks lived in cardboard and plywood shacks. Sanitation was impossible and people, especially the very young and very old, fell victim to all manner of diseases.

In the late 1920s a lot of folks kept a meat hog to fatten and kill; even in the towns. There was a man named Harv Fraley that went around and did the hog killing for a lot of folks. He would get the water just hot enough so you could swish your fingers through it without scalding them. He always said folks got the water too hot and would damage the meat. He had a wagon and an old truck and he would load up the carcasses and take them home to process the meat. Then he would deliver it back to the folks it belonged to. Harv was married to an English woman and they lived on a forty acre farm in the Frisco District. In the late 1920s, he bought a 1926 Ford Roadster. He and his wife would come to town in it with the top off. Mr. Fraley also dug a lot of wells in the area in the 1920s and 1930s. He managed to put back a little money and was one of the wealthier men around at the time.

PART 2: GROWING UP IN THE HARD TIMES

When Artie was eight years old, his grandpa took him out to a little cotton patch he had down by the orchard and taught him how to chop cotton. Chopping cotton "thinning it out" was a back breaking job. He also took Artie to the cow lot and taught him how to milk a cow. They had a little Jersey cow they called 'Bootsie 'and she was so gentle you could just plop down under her and go to milking. From that day on, Artie went to the cotton patch with everybody else to pick cotton. Sometimes it would come a big rain and be too muddy to get in the cotton patch, so most folks would take the opportunity to grab a fishing pole and wander down past Pilot Springs where the creek water would began to clear up and try to catch a mess of fish. Not if you lived with Ben Howard though. If it was too wet to work in the cotton fields, then he would put the boys to building fence or patching fence, or cutting wood. There was always work to be done and Ben didn't believe in wasting a good work day fishing.

When Artie was twelve years old, they had a cotton patch down on Pennington Creek. They were picking cotton down there one day and Artie was determined to pick 200 pounds of cotton. When it came time to quit, Ben hollered, "Let's go." Artie had 196 pounds of cotton. Didn't matter though, when Ben Howard said "Go," you went. Artie said Raymond turned out the same way. When he said "Go," Edith went.

When everybody had their crops all put away in the fall each year, it was then okay to turn your loose hogs out to run wherever they pleased and fend for themselves. There were a few rules everyone went by. First off, it must be assured that all crops were harvested so the hogs wouldn't damage anyone's crops. Secondly, the hogs must have rings in their noses to keep them from rooting and destroying good planting ground. Most everyone abided by the rules, but on occasion there would be misunderstandings.

One fall when all the crops were put away, Hub Bulman was having all kinds of problems with hogs rooting up his cotton fields. He finally determined the hogs belonged to Virgil Garrison. He knew Virgil had a pretty bad temper and Hub figured if he complained about the hogs, he would make him mad, so he wrote him a letter asking him to put rings in the hogs' noses. He made the mistake, however, of hand delivering the letter. Mr. Garrison told him that he figured the best way to handle the dispute was to just have a friendly fight to settle the issue. Hub, being a preacher, declined to take him up on the offer, but he later admitted that it really did make him mad when Virgil offered to fight him.

Hub Bulman would get up early on a Sunday morning and ride across country all the way to Wapanucka to conduct church services. Then he would ride back to Bellwood after the night service arriving home way up in the early hours of the morning.

Most everybody had an ice box. And when I say ice box, I mean ice box. That is just exactly what it was. A little later, propane refrigerators came to be common, but in the early 1900's and up into the late 1930s, most everybody had the plain old ice box. It was just an enclosed, cabinet-like fixture that had shelves in it and usually a lower and an upper door. The big block of ice went on the upper shelf. Cold air settles, so with the ice on the top shelf, the food on the lower shelves would get the cool air as it settled from the top.

The ice came from Sulphur in the back of an old truck. The blocks of ice would be covered with heavy layers of cloth to keep them from melting in the hot weather. The ice man usually came around every other day. If you didn't want your food to ruin, you had to be home when the ice man came around. If milk and cream were to be had, an extra block of ice would be bought on occasion and folks would make up a freezer of homemade ice cream.

Artie's Grandma Howard passed away when he was twelve years old. She was the only mother he ever knew, and although she was his grandma, he called her Mother just like her own kids did. She was the only person he had ever heard of to die from cancer. After she got sick, she started asking the kids to do more to help and one day she told Artie and Raymond to iron their overalls that had just been washed. They ironed for a little while, but Raymond allowed as how he'd ironed all he wanted to so he just quit ironing and sat down. She picked up a little switch she had laid close to hand and holding it where Raymond could see it, she told him he wasn't quitting until all the overalls were ironed. Raymond took her at her word and commenced to iron the overalls again. Artie just grinned and kept on ironing.

Times really changed around the Howard place after Martha's death. Ben Howard had never been a hand in the kitchen. You might see him sitting at the kitchen table reading the paper while Martha did the cooking, but you weren't apt to catch him trying to cook anything himself. In the two and a half years the Howard family lived in that house without the graces of a woman, they all learned to cook, wash their clothes, and keep the house in good order. It was a different way of life and it took everybody helping out to get things done.

After Leonard and Edith were married, they lived with Ben in the house on the old home place. Ben had a favorite chair in the living room and didn't take kindly to anyone sitting in his chair. One day he came into the house unannounced and found Leonard sitting in his chair with Edith in his lap.

"Well John Brown", he said. "I don't fancy anyone sitting in my chair and I come in and find two lovebirds in it. What's going on here anyway?"

Leonard and Edith hadn't been married long and Edith didn't quite know how to take it. She made a point though, to never sit in Ben's chair again.

In 1928, Ben Howard bought a little 1926 Ford car and

taught himself to drive. You didn't have to have a driver's license in those days. It was 1937 before a driver's license was required and then you didn't have to take a test, just tell them you intended to drive and they'd sell you a license.

Ben had a brother named Burn, and Burn remarked one day that he figured Ben must be looking at something 'cause he was wearing his necktie plum down to his belt buckle. Sure enough, it wasn't long before Ben came in one day and told Leonard's wife Edith that he was seeing someone and he wanted to bring her out and show her the place if Edith would cook dinner for her. Edith said she would, so Ben brought her out.

Ben Howard would marry the widow from Sulphur named Marie Thompson. Marie had never lived in the country, so it took her a little while to get acclimated. She was a good cook and a good housekeeper. When she moved to the Howard household, things changed again for the Howard children, Artie included. Artie was almost fifteen years old when Ben married Marie, and he lived with the Howards another five years.

Artie learned to plow with a team when he was 14 years old. They had a little cotton patch south of the Bellwood School House and one day Artie hitched up a team of mules, they called them "John and Pete," and his grandpa went with him over to the cotton patch. Ben set his plows for him and got him started down the row, but in no time Artie was fighting the plow trying to keep it out of the cotton row. "Well John Brown," Ben said. "If you'd keep them mules where they're supposed to be the plow will take care of itself.

Along about that time, there was a family that lived on a

forty acre allotment south of the Bellwood School House. The man's name was Nelson Colbert and he was half Indian and half black. Tom Cardwell later told Artie the story of how they came about getting the land. If a mixed blood would sign an affidavit declaring he was half Indian, the government would give him forty acres of land. That's how the Colbert family ended up on the forty acres south of the school house.

Nelson Colbert had a little mare he called "Strawhead" and she was a racing mare. He won a fair amount of money racing Strawhead in the shorter races of a quarter mile or less. He was also a good cowboy and won a lot of goat ropings. Artie saw him rope and tie a goat in under seven seconds at one roping.

Ab and Cecil Howard were about grown at that time and they happened by the Colbert place one summer night. They had a big fire going and were dancing around the fire and chanting some kind of song. Every once in a while, one of them would jump through the flames and keep on dancing. Jumping through the fire was supposed to run the devil off and cleanse you of bad spirits.

The Colbert family had an old lady living with them and they called her Grandma. It's not clear who's grandma she actually was. Anyhow, she died and they put her body in a wooden coffin. They loaded that coffin in a little wagon and hauled it with a team of mules all the way to Seeley Chapel north of Connerville and buried her. There were several of them along on the funeral trip and the only place there was to sit was on the coffin, so that's what they did. Several folks commented that they didn't think it was proper, but Artie said he didn't know what else they were supposed to do. He saw them go by when they left out and didn't think much about it one way or the other.

Artie would go and visit his Papa on occasion and stay a week or two. Artie's Papa Pierce married Nellie (Gaines-Conner) in 1923 when Artie was eleven years old. She had three boys when they married, Allen, Willie, and Rada. Everybody called Willie "Duter". She also had a daughter, Jettie, who died at a very young age. Nellie was a sister to Frank Gaines who married Emma Howard, so she seemed like a sister to Artie. Nellie and Pierce would eventually have four children of their own. Ruby, who married Harmon Clark, Obra Carl (they called him Sonny Boy), Betty who married Don Clark, and R.P. (Bub).

BOYS WILL BE BOYS

It was Christmas 1928 and as was the custom, the folks of the Bellwood Community were having their annual Christmas get together at the school house. It was an unseasonably warm night and the place was full. Folks were taking the opportunity to visit and get caught up on all the happenings around the area. With folks strung out across the district, and transportation being what it was, their busy schedules didn't always allow for the social graces. There were goodies to eat spread out on the tables across the front of the room and the smell of coffee brewing filled the air. The kids were all in a Holiday spirit and the sound of laughing voices mingled with the more serious talk of the adults.

The big Christmas tree stood in the corner by itself. It was a native red cedar, freshly cut by a couple of the bigger boys at the school. The kids had all helped decorate it, and the strings of popcorn were draped across the branches in sweeping rows around the tree. The tin foil ornaments sparkled as they picked up the light from the kerosene lanterns set in strategic locations throughout the room. There would be sacks of goodies for the kids to take home and enjoy. These would be passed out later as everyone was getting ready to go to their respective homes.

Out in front and spread around the south side of the building, were the various conveyances that brought the local folks to the festivities. Horses stood three legged at the hitch rails, wagons with their big draft horse teams were all together alongside the road leading to the schoolhouse. The lighter buggies and a carriage or two were nestled up close to the door of the school. There were two or three automobiles there, parked well away from the wagons so as not to spook the horses. There were forty or more families represented at the gathering that night.

Back inside the school house, the air was getting a little stuffy from the lanterns and the wood stove going strong in the back of the room. Someone thought it would be a good idea to crack a couple of windows to let in a little fresh air. It was about that time that Artie Quinton and his best buddy Elmore Garrison decided they would take a look around outside and get a little fresh air as well. As they walked around the side of the building, they could see through the windows as the smaller kids all gathered around the Christmas tree. They eased up alongside the building, right by the recently opened window where the Christmas tree stood. The tree had them hidden from the folks inside the building.

Now boys will be boys they say, and that hasn't changed much over the years. It's not clear which one started it but either Artie or Elmore reached through the open window, and grabbing a branch from the tree, began to shake the tree gently, then a little harder, until finally the whole tree was shaking and wobbling so hard that it was about to shed its array of ornaments right onto the floor. Kids started screaming and hollering, not knowing what was taking place, and men and women were hustling toward the tree to catch it before it toppled to the floor.

Outside the window, Artie and Elmore figured they had better find a more healthy environment, so they took off at a dead run across the school yard hoping they could get away before somebody spotted them. In the dark of the night, and with the excitement of the moment, neither of them remembered the clothesline wire running about five feet off the ground between the two posts at the side of the schoolyard. Elmore managed to avoid it, but Artie hit it at a high gallop and the wire caught him across the face leaving a raw cut from his chin, angling up across his cheek, all the way to his left ear. There wasn't time to tarry though, so he picked himself up off the ground and took off after Elmore, who by that time, was almost out of sight headed south as fast as he could run.

When they figured they were far enough away from the school to risk a light, Elmore scratched a match to life and for the first time he could see the damage the wire had done to Artie's face. The cool water from Pennington Creek helped the pain a little and they sat there on the creek bank trying to decide what to do. Finally, Elmore said the only thing he knew to do was to go to his house and let his Mother pray about it, so that's what they did. With a little cleaning and doctoring, and a little praying as well, the raw flesh was soon on its way to healing.

Hazel Garrison (Elmore's sister and now Hazel Cook) remembers the night Artie came to their house with the raw whelp across his face. She was just a little girl and didn't know what had happened, but that night has stuck in her mind over the years.

Innocent fun sometimes has a way of ending up a little differently than intended and such was the case in the Christmas tree incident. I can close my eyes, though and see Artie and Elmore giggling to each other as they shook the Christmas tree that night. A couple of buddies just having a little fun. They remained buddies throughout their lives.

I can see Elmore sitting on the very front pew of the church as he was prone to do. It was his very favorite spot, right up where he could hear everything the preacher had to say. I can still hear his "AMENS" as he followed along with the sermons. One of these days, he and Artie will be buddies together again in a much better place. Instead of shaking a Christmas tree, they will shake the hand of the Lord as He says "well done my true and faithful servants." I'm not sure if the Lord has a sense of humor, but if He does, He might even mention the Christmas tree incident. I want to be there to see it if He does.

In 1929, Artie went to Gotebo with Etta and Turner Pittman to pull bolls. He was sixteen when they left in August and turned seventeen that October. They were working for Alfred Pittman's family. Alfred and his wife had ten kids and also had a fellow by the name of Miley Jackson living with them. The pay was a dollar a hundred and Artie averaged a little over 200 pounds a day.

The strangest thing happened to Artie while he was at Gotebo. The folks that were pulling bolls would get mail from home occasionally and one day they brought some mail to Artie and it was all addressed to "Artie Quinton'. One of the pieces of mail was a letter addressed to him but when he started reading it, he couldn't relate to anything the letter talked about. It was like it was written to somebody else. Turned out, that's just what the problem was. The mail was addressed to him, but it wasn't his mail. There was a girl there pulling bolls and the mail belonged to her. Her name was Artie Quinton, spelled just like his name. He just gave her the mail and went about his business. He has wished all these years that he had questioned her about her name and how she came about it. At the time, being a sixteen year old kid, he was just too bashful to talk to her about it.

Over the next few years, Artie stayed and worked on the farm. About the only break from the work was an occasional trip to town with his best buddy Elmore Garrison. Along with Henry Pittman, they would eat an early breakfast and head to Mill Creek on horseback. Artie had a little paint mare that he rode for years and her name was Toni. He was real fond of that paint mare. The three of them would stay in town all day long, just hanging around. None of them had any money, so they would go without dinner. Along about sundown, they would ride the seven miles back home and eat supper.

One of the pastimes around Mill Creek in those days was the horse races. Horse racing was popular at the time and lots of folks had a horse they would race a little. Some guys would take a horse around the country and run races against the local favorites. You could nearly always bet they had a really fast horse or they wouldn't be taking him around to the races like they did. One young man around Mill Creek had a little mare that could really fly. He taught her to limp and he would bet with the guys that came through to race their horses. When they saw her limping, they figured it was a sure thing so they would get up a race and bet big against her. When she would line up at the starting line, the limp would magically disappear. She never lost a race.

Artie claims he never had a girlfriend he cared anything about until he met Agnes McClure. When I asked him about girlfriends and such as he went through his teenage years, he just smiled that Artie Quinton smile and changed the subject. I figured he had told me all he was going to about it, so we just moved on.

About the time he turned twenty, his Papa Pierce told him he would let him use 10 acres to put in a cotton crop if he wanted to move in with him. Not having any other prospects, he headed over to Pierce and Nellie's with about everything he owned on his back. He was leading a paint horse his papa had given him, but she got spooked and jerked away from him, so he didn't get there with her. The cotton crop came out fairly well that first year and he cleared around $100.00 which was a lot of money in those days for a single man to have.

After the crop was laid by, he was at loose ends again with really nothing to do and without any job prospects. He figured he could stay with his Papa and Nellie for as long as he wanted to, but he just didn't want to be a burden to them, so when

Frank Holly suggested they join the Navy, he said okay. Before they had a chance to go to the Navy Recruiting Station, Frank found out that you had to have a high school diploma to join. That shot that plan clean out of the saddle since neither of them had a high school education.

There were some good times along with the work that twenty months he stayed with his papa and Nellie. Folks managed to keep their sense of humor even in the lean times, it seemed. Nellie dearly loved to fish. She would sit on the creek bank for hours when she could find the time, with that old cane pole in her hand and the tin can of worms by her side. It was a good time to be alone and let the worries and stresses of everyday life just melt away.

One day as she sat and watched the cork bobbing along in the slow current, she thought she caught some movement out of the corner of her eye back up in the brush away from the creek. She had a feeling something was watching her, but every time she looked, there was nothing there. The feeling just wouldn't go away. Before long, she distinctly heard a noise behind her and to her right and as she turned that way to look, she spotted a colored man crouching in the brush just watching her. She could feel the fear building in her chest as she threw the pole down and headed for the house as fast as she could run. She was running across on old field between the creek and the house, and in her haste, she tripped and fell a number of times. By the time she reached the safety of the house, both knees and elbows were skinned and bloody as was the palms of her hands where she skidded on the dirt.

Before long, the ***"colored"*** man opened the door and

stepped into the living room. He was wiping the black from his face as he stepped in the door. It was none other than Turner McKinney. He had taken charcoal from the stove and blackened his face to look like he was a colored man, then sneaked down to the creek to scare her. Nellie was as mad as an old wet hen, and Turner had to vacate the premises to get away from her. He said later, if he would have known it was going to scare her so badly, he probably wouldn't have done it.

There was a novel way to get the County work accomplished during the early part of the 20th century. I'm not sure how long the practice was in place, but it was a period of several years at least. The "free work program" for the County was going strong at the time and Artie would put in his time and then he would put in his papa's time too. You had to do it once a year. If you had a team of horses or mules, and could work with a team, you had to put in two days free work grading roads or doing some other work for the County with the team. If you didn't have a team, you had to put in four days as a single worker. The County had no laborers, so this was the way the County work got done. At one time, Will Quinton, my grandpa and Arties uncle, was a crew boss for the free labor workers and would assign jobs for them to do across the County. Many of the ranches and other businesses that employed workers would assign one person to put in the equivalent time for all the employees that worked at that particular business. In that manner, they could maintain a stable work force, and the County fared better because they always had experienced workers to do the County work. If a business employed enough workers, it took a person working full time for the County to fulfill the requirement for all the businesses employees.

PART 3: LOVE AT FIRST SIGHT

The McClure exodus from the Drake/Nebo Community to Mill Creek occurred in 1933. Robert (Bob) and Nancy McClure, (Ag's parents), along with Pete and Eula McClure and Bess and Bill Cook all moved to the Mill Creek area with their families. Pete and Bess were Ag's brother and sister. Ag was the youngest of eleven children born to Bob and Nancy and was sixteen years old when she moved to Mill Creek and met the love of her life. The first time she saw Artie Quinton, they were walking to church. Most folks walked to church in those days, and Artie, dressed up in a wine colored jacket with blue collar and cuffs, caught her eye. She had a friend named Fanny Strange visiting from Drake and Butch Bray liked her looks so he thought he'd ask her out. It went something like this.

"How about we go out on a date, Fanny?" Butch asked.

Not knowing Butch, Fanny looked over at Ag to get her reaction.

"You aren't going to turn down a deal like that are you?" Ag replied.

Artie, standing close by, overheard the exchange, and gathering up his nerve, thought he'd make his play as well.

"Would you turn down a deal like that with me Ag?" he asked.

"Why don't you try me?" she replied.

That started a relationship that would last more than sixty-three years. They mostly dated just walking to church. Wasn't much else to do, and not much way to go anywhere if there had been someplace to go. As the weeks turned into months, and the months into years, the relationship blossomed and they began to talk of marriage. Artie always said she had the prettiest legs of any woman he ever saw.

Only two problems: there was no job and no place to live. Neither of them wanted to have to live with anyone else, so the wedding bells would just have to wait. Ag wanted to finish school anyway; she wanted to be a school teacher. She had been staying with her uncle in a little place called Council Hill, east of Henrietta and going to school. She had a sister that was really sick with cancer and she finally died in the hospital at Oklahoma City. Ag was a junior in high school at Council Hill, but she figured her mother might need her after her sister died, so she came home and went the spring semester of her junior year at Mill Creek. The young couple dated through the spring and summer, then Ag went back to Council Hill for her senior year, graduating in the spring of 1934. When she left for Council Hill in the late summer of 1933, Artie promised to come visit her just as soon as his cotton crop was put by. True to his word, he and Arvel Pitmon borrowed Richard Pitmon's car and drove up there to see her. Jo McClure, Ag's sister went with them. She would later marry Arvel. They stayed a couple of nights with Pete McClure and his family, and Ag showed them around and introduced them to her classmates. Pete made a good living raising and baling hay in the Council Hill area for many years.

The whole country was in a severe drought that spring and summer of 1934. The depression was in full swing and there were no jobs to be had. Cattle and sheep were not worth much, it was difficult to even find a place to sell them for anything at all. The stockyards at Oklahoma City were full of cattle and trucks were backed up just waiting to get a chance to unload. Harry Thompson drove one hundred head of cattle down to a place on his ranch they called 'Pecan Holler' and just shot them. They wouldn't bring anything at the sale, and the grass was all burned up. There is no telling how many cattle were shot in 1933 and 1934. It was too dry to plant anything, so what was a young fellow to do?

There was a man named Oat Smith that worked at the First State Bank in Tishomingo around the time when the depression was at its height. He never owned a car and would ride a horse to the bank to work every morning. He was in charge of all transactions at the bank that had anything to do with livestock. Any money that was loaned on livestock had to be approved by Oat Smith. Oat was a brother to Tom and Clint Smith who lived West of Reagan Oklahoma for many years.

The meeting place around the Bellwood area in the early 1930s was at Tom Clement's place. They had a regular sale there every week and folks would bring livestock over there to sell. Oat Smith was the official expert on what livestock was worth and he would set the price when someone would bring in livestock to sell. The folks from Mill Creek and around would come up there and buy cattle. It was about the time pressure cookers came into existence and folks would buy the beef for little or nothing and take it home and can it. Artie said he remembered it being really tasty.

When Billy Pittman was growing up in the Mill Creek area, his father Earl Pittman was good friends with Artie. Artie is about 18 years older than Billy, so was in his twenties by the time Billy was old enough to remember him. Billy told me a story his father had related to him about a time in the early 1930's when Earl and Artie were making a trip over to Hobart Oklahoma. It's not clear what the nature of their business in Hobart was, but they were in a Model "A" and it had rained quite a bit earlier in the day. About six or seven miles before they got into Hobart they ran across a man whose car had slid off in the ditch. The roads were all dirt roads at the time and when it rained, the red clay would get really slick.

The fellow flagged them down and asked if they would pull him out of the ditch. They didn't have a chain, but they did have two lariat ropes in the car. They wouldn't hardly go anywhere without their ropes. They doubled up the ropes to make sure they wouldn't break and commenced to pull the old car out of the ditch. The back wheels of that Model "A" was slinging mud everywhere, but they finally managed to pull the car out onto the road. When they got straightened out on the road, they decided they might as well have some fun so they just took off down the road dragging the car behind them. The man was hollering for them to stop, but they just kept on going as fast as they could go and still keep the model "A" in the road. He'd slam on the brakes occasionally, but every time he did, the old car would start sliding toward the ditch. They slung mud all the way to town and by the time they pulled up and stopped at a service station on the outskirts of Hobart, the front of the fellow's old car was covered with mud. The space between the grill and radiator was filled with mud, and the windshield was covered with the stuff.

The fellow was mad as a hornet but was even more scared then he was mad. He couldn't see a thing through the mud covered windshield, so he had to hold his head out of the window part of the time to see where he was going. His hair and face were both covered with mud, and his eyes were as big as silver dollars. Earl and Artie untied their ropes from the bumper of the old car and eased out of there as quickly as they could. As the Model "A" headed off down the street, the sound of their laughter floated back to where the fellow was busily trying to get enough mud off the car so he could continue on his way. I'll bet he thought twice before he asked for help again.

THE STORM OF 1933

It was a Thursday afternoon May 11, 1933 and it hit as they were eating supper. It was on them before they knew it. It blew George Burk's house away and headed for Pierce and Nellie Quinton's place. The sky had begun to get dark, the clouds looked bad, and Nellie wanted to go to the cellar. Frank Gaines, Ott McDonald, Mutt Garrison, and Artie were all at Pierce and Nellie's house. Mutt was twelve years old and Artie was twenty at the time. Finally, Ott told Nellie he would go to the cellar with her and the kids.

They had no more than got into the cellar when the whole house started shaking. The washtubs had already blown off the side of the house where Nellie had hung them on the nails like always. Nellie had just recently hired Willie Garrison to hang wallpaper on some of the walls in the house. That wallpaper started coming off the walls in sheets. Pierce was trying to close the front door, but every time he would almost get it closed, the wind would blow it open again. Artie and Mutt were going from room to room, not sure what to do.

"What in the hell are we going to do now," Mutt wanted to know.

"This sure ain't no time to be using that kind of language," Frank told him.

That really got Mutt's attention. About that time, the smokehouse blew away. Shingles were flying off the house in every direction. The air was filled with debris in every direction you could see. Then the porch tore loose from the house and smashed into pieces. Finally, the wind started to die down and the tornado moved on in an easterly direction.

Leon Seeley lived about a quarter of a mile from George and Jewel Burk's place and he saw their house blow away. He knew he had to get to Pierce's house to let him know what had happened. It was just a short distance across the pasture and over the creek to their house. Pennington Creek was running out of its banks, however, from all the rain, so he had to walk around the road and across the bridge to get to Pierce's house to tell them what had happened over at the Burks. George and Jewell Burk were Artie's Uncle and Aunt. Jewell was Artie's father's sister. ***(Author's note: She was also a sister to my grandpa, Will Quinton.)*** They went over to Everett Bray's to get him to drive them over there in his car. Everett had an old Dodge car and they piled up in it and headed over to the Burk's. They got stuck several times but managed to push the old car out each time.

When they arrived, they found that Aunt Jewel was the

only one that was mobile. Paul Burk was in the cellar. Aunt Jewell had managed to get him into the cellar after the tornado was gone. It was the only place left to put him with the house blown away. She had found him lying in a pile of scrap metal and the top of his head was peeled back. It looked like a lister plow point or something like that had hit him in the head. Nobody could figure out how she managed to get him into the cellar and she didn't know either.

Artie's Grandma Quinton was sitting between the cellar and where the house used to be. Aunt Jewel had helped her to sit up, but she had her arm out to brace herself. She most certainly had internal injuries and probably a broken hip, but she was praying as loud as she could pray. She was happy and praying to the Lord. She had on an old gingham dress, and if she had any money, she had it pinned inside her apron pocket. ***(author's note: Artie's Grandma Quinton was my great grandma.)***

Paul Burk had a 1928 "A" model Ford, and it was parked on the north side of the house. There was a little dog tied to the bumper of the car. Neither the car or the dog were hurt. They loaded Uncle George, Paul, and Grandma Quinton into the car and pushed it down the hill and over to Sallie Gaddis's house. Grandma Quinton lived a few days but ultimately died of the injuries she received in the tornado. She died on May 15th 1933 and is buried in the Mill Creek cemetery. She was 68 years old.

A doctor came out there from somewhere and sewed Paul's head up. He must have thought he was going to die, because he didn't even clean the dirt out of the wound, he just sewed it up. Tom Clement and Gouhl Holder came over there in Tom's four door Model "A". They loaded Paul up and took him to Ardmore to the hospital. He would have surely died had they not done that. He was in the hospital for several weeks, and when he was released, he had to learn to do everything all over again. He had to crawl until he learned to walk again. He was just learning to do things again like a baby would. He finally recovered fully and worked with Artie in the feed pens a few years later.

Uncle George had some burns around his head and neck area. He was lying in a fence row when Aunt Jewel found him and his hair was on fire. Nobody knew how the fire started, but speculated it must have been from lightening hitting the ground. It might even have hit Uncle George.

It was the worst storm to hit the area in anybody's memory. It went on north and east from the Quinton place. It damaged Roy Quinton's barn and did significant damage to the Bellwood School House. It was in the air by then, or it would have destroyed both structures. There was someone else who went through that storm, but she wasn't aware of it at the time. Aunt Jewell Burk was pregnant at the time, and her daughter Dorothy was born eight and a half months later. That makes her a survivor of the big storm of 1933.

PART 4: THE ARMY YEARS

1934-1937

In the summer of 1934, the Army began to look like as good an option as any to Artie. Seems like there was just no end to the problems. If he was going to join the Army, he would have to somehow get to the Army Recruiting Station, and that was located on the third floor of the Post Office Building in Oklahoma City. A few days later, he learned that Cecil Howard was hauling a trailer load of cattle to the Oklahoma City Stockyards for Corn Clark, so Artie caught a ride with him. They had a trailer load of Jersey steers behind the truck and the old trailer was connected to the truck with a mechanism sort of like a coupling pin on a wagon. They hadn't gotten very far when they hit a low place and the pin came loose. The trailer load of steers took off across the ditch and came to rest in the pasture. The steers scattered all over the country and it took a while to gather them back up. A few days later, they set out again, this time with Corn Clark following behind in the car in case something else happened.

When they finally arrived at the stock yards and unloaded the steers, Corn Clark asked Artie where he was headed.

"Well, I want to go to the Army Recruiting Station. I know where it is, but I don't know how to get there," Artie replied.

"Where is it located?" he asked.

"It's supposed to be on the third floor of the post office," Artie said.

"Get in and I'll take you there," he said. "I know right where it is."

When they arrived at the post office, Artie bid him farewell and climbed the three flights of stairs to the third floor. Sure enough, there was a sign on the door that said "Army Recruiting Station", but there was no one in the room. He took a chair and waited awhile and finally a man came in and asked him what he wanted.

"I'd like to join the Army," he said.

"Well, fill out this here form and I'll be right back." The man handed him a mental test form and walked out the door. By the time the man returned, Artie had the form filled out so he just handed it to him. The man looked over the form and said it looked alright and guessed he passed. "Do you really want to join the Army?" he asked.

"I sure do," Artie replied. "I don't have a job and I don't have any money."

"Well, there are at least a hundred men ahead of you," the man said. "Lots of guys trying to get into the Army. You look like a good young man though. Tell you what; if you really want to get in the Army, I believe I can get you in maybe as early as two weeks. Let's go ahead and get you a physical while you're here." For some reason, the recruiter took a liking to Artie and thought he'd help him out. Artie has that effect on a lot of folks. They walked down the street about five blocks to a clinic and Artie was able to go ahead and get his physical taken care of. Now it was just a matter of waiting until the recruiter called.

Artie joined the Army on August 27th 1934. They swore him in at Oklahoma City and he was sent to Ft. Sill, Oklahoma, over by Lawton. There were only three men sworn in that day. One of the men who went with him from Oklahoma City to Ft. Sill was a man named Austin Depth. Austin was a Cherokee Indian from Sallisaw, Oklahoma and he had been trying to get into the Army for a year or more. He'd been staying with his sister in Oklahoma City 'til he could get in. The other man was Douglas Blair and he was originally from Indiana.

The Military Police met them at Ft. Sill and took them to the barracks. The 77th field artillery had just been formed and new barracks were built to house them. That's where Artie spent his first night in the Army. It was a little scary; he hadn't seen but two men in uniform in his entire life until he got to Ft. Sill. He remembered seeing his papa in uniform when he came back from World War 1, and he had seen Roy Quinton's brother-in-law in a uniform one time. When he got to Ft. Sill, there were men in uniform everywhere he looked.

The Army pay when he joined up was $21.00 a month. They took $1.50 out of his check to launder his clothes, and he gave a little to the Old Soldiers Fund, so his take home pay was between $18.00 and $19.00 a month. There were WW1 veterans still in the Army at Ft. Sill. There just weren't any jobs for them on the outside, so they just stayed in the Army to have something to do and make a little money. Artie spent the next three years at Ft. Sill.

Artie in his Army uniform in either **1935** *or* **1936**

The second day right after roll call, the three new recruits were assigned their units. The regular drill sergeant was on furlough in Arkansas and so another sergeant they called Sergeant David worked with them a few days just showing them the rudimentary steps, like "Left, right, left" and "about face" and that sort of thing. When the Drill Sergeant returned, it was easy to see why he was a drill sergeant. He was a tough looking man, had spent some time in the Philippines, and was middle weight boxing champion while he was over there. His name was Buck Wells.

The first day they drilled with Sergeant Wells, he lined them up. "Is there anybody here in this group that thinks he's tough?" He asked. Nobody stepped out.

"I just thought if somebody thought he was a tough guy, I'd just pull these stripes off and we'd get that settled right up front."

After they got settled in and started drilling on a regular basis, Artie grew to like Sergeant Wells. He was a good man and a good soldier. Sergeant Wells had a regular sergeant over him and everybody called him Sergeant Johnny. One day they had the post band playing and they were drilling out in front of the barracks and Sergeant Johnny came running out of one of the buildings.

"Stop that marching right now," he bellowed. "You can't get these guys to marching the way they're supposed to with that band. They're so out of tune nobody could march to their playing." So they got an unexpected rest.

Sergeant Wells asked Artie if he knew anything about horses and he said he did, so they assigned him to the mounted patrol unit. They had a little different way of riding and working horses in the Army than what he was used to. The Army had some regulations about how you rode, how fast you rode, and even how you sat a horse. You had to get in rhythm with the horse as you rode. They called it "posting". Artie caught on to that pretty quick. One other regulation they had was the way you warmed up a horse. You had to keep the horse in a walk for at least a mile before you got up into a trot. The Army figured it took at least a mile of walking for a horse to get his blood circulating all through his body. If you didn't get him warmed up this way, he might injure himself, they figured. It didn't matter what the weather was like, you had to exercise all the horses at least every other day. Artie rode all over the mountains around Ft. Sill. Most of the time, he would ride one horse and lead two more.

The men in the horse unit were assigned to the 18th Field Artillery and they ate with them and everything. They didn't have their own battery so they would sleep on the third floor of whatever battery they happened to be assigned to at the time. The headquarters building was on the third floor over the barracks. Artie had just been assigned to communications school. At that time every post had a boxing club and one of the other soldiers talked Artie into trying out for the club. Now Artie had been working pretty hard before he joined the Army and was in really good shape. He didn't know anything about boxing; he just knew you had to throw leather if you were going to win.

He was boxing a guy one day and was really laying the leather to his opponent. Everybody was hollering and clapping and when the fight was over, they gave him a standing ovation. A little later, one of the guys told Artie that Sergeant Scruggs, ***(they called him Old Woosy Brushy)***, was outside and wanted to talk to him. He went outside and the sergeant told him he had been watching him box and he had as much nerve as he'd ever seen.

The 18th Field Artillery had a man by the name of Wilson

that could really box and Sergeant Scruggs thought he had a really good chance of being Post Middleweight Champion, but he needed somebody that could box to spar with him every day.

"Tell you what I want you to do," Sergeant Scruggs said. "Every day when you go in for lunch, instead of going to your afternoon duty, you go to the gym and work out with Wilson. I mean for you to really lay the leather to him." So that's what he did until the boxing championships took place. The 18th Field Artillery won three Post Boxing Championships that year. It was the best year they ever had.

There was an old Lieutenant named Bilchoe on the post and he was an Irishman. He would walk around on the post and if you met up with him you had to remember to salute him. He was of the old school, and if you didn't follow protocol around him, you might end up with extra duty or something. He did have a funny saying though. He'd say it every time after you saluted him. ***"By the dung of a royal horse, what good have you done for your country today?"*** It was a funny saying, and he would say it every time without fail. He had an old car and he was having a lot of trouble with it. One day he couldn't get it to start so he just pulled his Forty-Five and shot it through the radiator. I guess that showed the thing who was the boss.

If you are in the Army very long, you are going to have guard duty. That's just the way it is. One night, Artie was Corporal of the Guard, and was standing guard duty when the Guard Sergeant came walking up to him. About the time he saw him coming Artie realized he didn't have the top button on his shirt buttoned. Sure enough, that's the first thing the sergeant spotted.

"Have you ever been on guard duty before?" He asked.

"Yes sir," Artie replied.

"Why don't you have the top button on your shirt buttoned?" He asked. "Is it too tight to button?"

"Yes sir," Artie replied.

"Well that's a good excuse, but I don't believe it," the sergeant said. With that, he turned and walked off. Artie breathed a sigh of relief. It's not often you get by with that sort of thing.

Not everybody is cut out for the Army, and not everything goes well either. In the three years Artie was at Ft. Sill, there were two attempted suicides. The only firearm that the soldiers carried was a Forty-Five. The Forty-Five pistols were real bad to jump when you fired them unless you squeezed the shot off. A walking guard had all he could take one night and he decided to end it all by shooting himself through the heart. The gun jumped on him though and he shot himself above the heart. He spent a long time in the hospital, then was discharged. Another soldier decided to cut his wrist. He was discovered and taken to the hospital ward before he died. Artie saw the sheets from his bed and they were really bloody. That soldier was discharged as well.

There was a Polish soldier by the name of Jericho that was a leather man and he was a married man. He was assigned to take care of the saddles and leather goods for the horse unit. He talked with a really strong Polish accent. There was a fair amount of gambling and the like that took place on the post. There really wasn't much to do in the way of entertainment. The "day room" was the place they all hung out when off duty and it had a couple of pool tables and some card and domino tables scattered around. The "day room," in fact all the barracks area, was for the men only and women were strictly forbidden inside. Jericho was in there one night gambling and in walked his wife and grabbed him up by the scruff of the neck and hauled him out of there. A couple of days later some of the guys saw him and thought they'd hurrah him a little about the episode.

"Hey Jericho," they hollered. "Your woman kind of showed you who was boss the other night didn't she?"

"Yea," he said. "She's an Englishman, temper higher than hell."

In those days, most battalions had prayer before they ate every meal. The same old sergeant would pray every time they ate. It was also a tradition to have a beer party on a regular basis. Some would drink and some wouldn't. They would have a meal and then the beer party would follow after the meal. One of the soldiers had just gotten a "Dear John" letter from his girlfriend that very afternoon. He sat quietly as the sergeant prayed over the meal. When the sergeant finally finished, he couldn't hold it back any longer. "If you're through praying, pass the beer," he said.

Normal supper time was at 5:00 o'clock in the afternoon on the base. Most nights, a lot of guys would be hungry again before bedtime. There was a Chinese family on base that ran a little eatery, and you could get chili and beans, maybe some cornbread, and always ice cream. Some of the guys would go over there and get a snack most every night. The Chinese folks were not Army, so must have been contracted out as a vendor to the Army. That little eatery sure saved a lot of soldiers from going to bed hungry on a lot of occasions.

There was no money allocated for promotions, so enlisted men were pretty much stuck in whatever rank they were in until the economy got better. There was one exception to the rule and Artie fell into that exception. Since there were no funds available to pay for promoting him to the rank of Corporal, he was promoted to "Acting Corporal" until such time that funding became available to pay for the extra pay that went with the promotion. Supposedly, the pay and the promotion would both be retroactive when the money was approved. To make it official, Artie was given a black armband with a first class chevron sewed to it that signified he was an "Acting Corporal." When the funding for promotions finally came about, he got the raise alright, but the back pay never came through.

The only time Artie ever got called onto the carpet for anything was when he was "Day Room Orderly." He had been up early on some kind of a problem and was working until 11:00 o'clock at night as "Day Room Orderly." You watched over the day room and collected the pool table money and whatever. You got to keep 10% of the take for running the day room. The take would usually run around $50. Since he had been working since early in the morning and was tired, Artie figured since it was a slow night anyway, he'd just close up early. He ended up taking in around $20. The next day, the battery clerk came in and told him the Captain wanted to see him. When he got over to the Captain's Office, the Captain told him to sit down.

"Quinton," he said. "You was a right smart light on your money last night. What happened?"

"Well, I had a problem call early that morning and it was slow that night. Not many guys playing pool, so I just shut down early," Artie replied.

"Son," the captain said. "Do you realize that when you signed up for the Army that you committed to work 24 hrs. a day if need be?"

"Yes sir," Artie replied. He didn't close up early any more after that incident.

On February 6th 1937, he came home on leave from the Army and he and Ag got married. Ag was afraid he wouldn't get his leave so she hadn't told anyone they were going to get married. When she left the house that day, she told her sister she might not be back home. "If I don't come back home, tell Mama and Papa I got married." She was twenty years old at the time, so didn't figure they were going to get too excited about her running off to get married. She told Artie not to worry; her parents always cared more for him than they did her anyway.

His Aunt, Emma Gaines, and her husband Frank took Ag to Sulphur to meet him at the bus station. Ag went to Greens Department Store to buy a new dress, but she didn't have anywhere to iron it so she just wore what she had on. They went to St. Paul's Methodist parsonage to get married. The preacher, Brother Payne, had been working on the railroad and had just got home from work. "Give me twenty minutes to clean up and change clothes," he said. "Then I'll marry you." Frank and Emma served as witnesses.

The newly married couple stayed with Frank and Emma that night and the next morning when they got up, Frank grinned at them. "How do you two devils like sleeping with each other," he said. It was a little embarrassing, but you had to expect something like that from Frank, he was quite a mess.

Ag had acquired a bedroom suite and Frank and Emma had been keeping it for them. They didn't tell anyone who it belonged to, so folks thought it belonged to Frank and Emma. Several families bought new bedroom suites as well. You know how it is, if the Joneses get something new, the Smiths have got to have one too. When they figured out it belonged to Artie and Ag, there were a few sheepish looks going around.

The honeymoon was short lived, and Artie returned to Ft. Sill to finish out his stint in the Army. He would be discharged from the Army in August, 1937 and arrived back in Mill Creek on August 26th.

The day he left, all his buddies gathered around and slapped him on the back and wished him well. It was sort of like leaving home for him. A man can develop some good friendships over a period of three years and it was hard to leave those friendships behind. One of his buddies drove him into Lawton so he wouldn't have to take the bus.

Twenty years later, he went to a reunion of the 18th Field Artillery at Ft. Sill and got to see some of the guys again. It was the last time he saw most of them.

Honorable Discharge

from

The Army of the United States

TO ALL WHOM IT MAY CONCERN:

This is to Certify, That* Artie Quinton
†6258219, Corporal, Hq & Hq Battery, 2nd Bn., 18th F.A.
THE ARMY OF THE UNITED STATES, as a TESTIMONIAL OF HONEST AND FAITHFUL SERVICE, is hereby HONORABLY DISCHARGED from the military service of the UNITED STATES by reason of‡ Expiration of Service.

Said Artie Quinton was born in Mill Creek, in the State of Oklahoma

When enlisted he was 21 9/12 years of age and by occupation a Farmer

He had Brown eyes, Brown hair, Ruddy complexion, and was 5 feet 7 inches in height.

Given under my hand at Fort Sill, Oklahoma this 26th day of August, one thousand nine hundred and Thirty-Seven

E. S. [illegible]

Colonel, 18th F.A.
Commanding.

See A.R. 345-470.
* Insert name; as, "John J. Doe."
† Insert Army serial number, grade, company, regiment, and arm or service; as "1620302"; "Corporal, Company A, 1st Infantry"; "Sergeant, Quartermaster Corps." 2—3164
‡ If discharged prior to expiration of service, give number, data, and source of order or full description of authority therefor.

W. D., A. G. O. Form No. 55
December 1, 1936

Artie's Honorable Discharge from the Army

AGNES MCCLURE QUINTON

One thing for certain about a man who has lived with and loved a woman for most of his life is that he has been shaped, to some degree, by her philosophies, her dreams, and her beliefs. To fully understand a man, you must also understand the woman who stands beside him. The woman who, through thick and thin, has stood with him for better and for worse throughout the years. She has shared his dreams, his successes, and his failures. She has rejoiced with him, cried with him, and prayed ***with*** him and ***for*** him. She has borne his children, and made a home wherever he chose to be. She has nurtured the flame of their love and made the welfare of the family the most important thing in her life.

And so it was with Agnes Quinton. I could not do justice to Artie's biography without also writing of Ag, her history, and her influence on his life. Although you will find her included throughout the chapters and stories of this book, I wanted also to chronicle her life in a separate way. Some of the data and information, by necessity, may be redundant, but I felt it was important to record her contributions to his life in this manner.

Agnes McClure was born the youngest of eleven children to Robert (Bob) and Nancy McClure. The date was November 30th, 1916. Her ten siblings and a short history of each are as follows.

Claude and Maude (twins) were born in April 30, 1894. Ag really never got to know Claude since he was the oldest and she was the youngest. He left home when she was a week old. Claude died May 14 1960. Maude passed away December 12, 1932 at the young age of 38 years. She died of cancer in Oklahoma City and is buried at Drake, Oklahoma.

John was born February 4, 1896 and died July 19, 1962. John married Florence Ross and they had two sons, Jack and Buddy. Jack was two years younger than Ag.

Bessie was born November 23, 1898 and died June 21, 1969. She married Bill Cook and they had two sons James and Horace. James died at a young age and Horace attends the Mill Creek Pentecostal Holiness Church with his wife Hazel today. Horace and Hazel have three sons.

Lizzie was born September 1, 1901 and died November 23, 1992. She married Clayburn Roundtree and they had five children, Jimmy Ray, Milburn, Wilburn, Bobby, and Odessa. Jimmy Ray was killed in World War 1.

Jim was born February 23, 1905 and died May 22, 1968. He married Clara Brewer and they had two sons, Billy and James. James was called" Sonny."

Lee was born April 25, 1907 and died March 8, 1964. He was injured years earlier in a wreck while working for Hicks Hardware store in Sulphur, and died from complications resulting from the wreck. He married Syble Sweeten and they had two daughters, Quannah, and Maudie. Quannah worked with her dad and helped him bale hay.

Pete was born February 27, 1909 and died December 13, 1984. He married Eula Bow and they had five children, James Dow, Repete, Ramona, Sharon, and Bobby. ***(Author's Note: Bobby was a year older than me and we went to school and played ball together. Bobby graduated in 1965 from Mill Creek High School and I graduated the following year.)***

Jessie was born May 27, 1911 and died February 10, 1986. She had four children, Erma Lou, Joyce, Robert, and Tommie. Jessie would give you the shirt off of her back, or the shirt off of somebody else's back if it was handy. She once borrowed a couple of Ag's dresses and when Ag finally got around to asking about them, Jessie said a woman really needed them so she gave them to her. "I knew you wouldn't mind," she said.

Jo was born April 5, 1914 and died November 21, 1949 at the age of 35 years. She married Arvel Pitmon and they had three daughters, Wanda, Bonnie, and Arvella. Wanda was 14, Bonnie 12, and Arvella 8 when their mother passed away. Ag and Jo were really close in age and were really close as sisters. Ag just felt like she didn't have anything left to live for when Jo died. Before she died, Jo would go to Artie and Ag's house to wash clothes and she would hide Bonnie among the clothes and tell Janet that she didn't come. After Jo died, Artie and Ag helped Arvel with the girls and they always felt like the girls were theirs. The girls always sent them Mother's Day and Father's Day cards.

Carol Daube Sutton was always fond of Ag and good to her when they lived on the ranch. Carol was Leon Daube's sister. She would call and ask Ag what she needed. One time she called and after they talked awhile, she asked Ag if she needed anything for the house. Ag had her heart set on one of the new Kirby vacuum cleaners. She told Mrs. Sutton she would like to have a new vacuum cleaner. Mrs. Sutton asked her what kind she wanted and what did she figure it would cost. Ag had done some checking around, and she had found one for $600.00. Mrs. Sutton told her to go ahead and get it and just sign the bill. When Ag went to get the Kirby, she found they had gone up in price and were now over $700.00. She told the man she'd take it, but she would sign the bill for $600.00 and write a check for the balance. Mrs. Sutton never knew about it. She would have gladly paid the entire price, and Ag knew she would, but she just didn't feel right about doing that. That episode describes pretty well, the kind of woman she was.

Agnes McClure Quinton went to be with her Lord on July 25, 2000. She grew up in the Drake Community and her family moved to the Mill Creek area in 1933. She attended High School in Council Hill, Oklahoma where she stayed with her uncle Pete McClure. He was her dad's brother. She graduated in the spring of 1934. She married Artie Otto Quinton on February 6, 1937. The first time she saw him she said, "That's my man." She and Artie had one daughter, Janet born March 24, 1945. Ag worked alongside her husband Artie from the time he started working for Daube Ranch on September 1st, 1937 until he retired in 1984.

She worked for the County Election Board for 38 years starting in 1938. She was an excellent cook and homemaker. She probably cooked more meals for cowboys over the years than the old time chuck wagon cooks of the cattle drive days. Ag's relationship with God was a special thing for her. When she accepted the Lord as her personal savior, she told Artie there were three things she wanted them to do; pay tithes, thank God for their food, and have family prayer at night. She was a positive influence on Artie's live and he was saved a year or so after Ag gave her life to God.

Artie and Ag bought a lot in town from Daubes in 1964 and built a home to retire to when the time was right. They rented it out until Artie retired in 1984. The house was 24 foot by 44 foot, a three bedroom, one bath home. The total cost of the construction was $5,066. Butch Fires added a garage on later. Artie lives there today.

Agnes Quinton was a strong woman. Her fortitude, her

work ethic, and her determination are reminiscent of the pioneer spirit that embodied the women that forged a way of life that is fast disappearing in our nation today. She married a cowboy, and she nurtured that cowboy into the kind of man that commands the friendship and respect of everyone he knows and meets to this very day. Artie Quinton is known to be a man of God. Agnes McClure Quinton contributed in large part to what that man became and is today.

PART 5: WORKING AT THE FEED LOT

Richard Pitmon had run across Ag a few days before Artie was due home from the Army and told her that Daube's Ranch was going to be hiring a couple to work in the feedlot on September 1st. The woman would have to do the cooking for the feedlot crew and the man would work in the feedlot. Ag, knowing Artie would need a job, went to see her father-in-law Pierce Quinton whom she knew was a good friend of Jude Kingsberry, the foreman at the ranch.

"Daube Ranch is going to hire a man to run the feedlot," she said. "Supposed to start on September 1st. Artie is coming home on the 26th of August. If you would go and talk to Jude, he might give Artie the job." So Pierce talked to Jude and Jude told him to have Artie call him when he got home. When Artie arrived, he went to his papa's and called out to the ranch, but

Jude was asleep. He called a couple of times, but caught Jude asleep both times. When Jude finally finished his nap, he drove down to Pierce and Nellie's and they sat on the porch and visited for a while. Finally the conversation got around to the job.

"Was you wanting to talk to me about a job, Artie?" Jude asked.

"I sure was," Artie replied.

"Well, tell you what," Jude said. "You come out to the ranch tomorrow at 1:00 o'clock. Mr. Cardwell, the General Manager, will be there and we'll talk about it then."

When Artie and Ag got to the ranch the next afternoon, they found Jude and Mr. Cardwell leaning up against the pump house talking. They just told it like it was going to be.

"This is going to be a hard job," Mr. Cardwell said. "Seven days a week and the wife will have to do the cooking."

"I can cook alright," Ag replied. "All I know though is just plain cooking"

"That's all you'll have to cook," Mr. Cardwell replied with a grin. "Just so there's plenty of it. Tell you what we'll do. If you want to try it, I'll give you $30.00 a month for the both of you."

They agreed, shook hands and started to leave, but they hadn't gotten back out to the car when Mr. Cardwell hollered at them.

"Here's what we're going to do," he said. " I'll have to knock the regular hands back a quarter a day, but I'm going to give you $35.00 a month."

That was a seventeen percent raise without even starting to work. Can't beat a deal like that. When Chester Belcher learned that his pay was getting cut a quarter a day, he just got mad and quit. His daddy gave him ten dollars to go back out to the feed pens and get his old job back, so he did. Chester was dating Veta Mary at the time and he would work all day, eat supper, and then ride a horse six miles to Mill Creek to see her.

The little house Artie and Ag moved into, (the first house they shared in their married life) was a little house made out of ship-lap boards an inch thick and six inches wide just stood up on a boxboard floor and nailed together. There was not even a step at the door, you just walked up to the wall, opened the door, and stepped into the house. With the men working in the feedlot coming in and out that door all day, it was a constant job just to keep the floors mopped. The house was ten foot wide and thirty foot long, and was divided up into three ten foot by ten foot rooms. Artie and Ag were in the north room, the middle room served as a kitchen, and the south room housed three cowboys. The kitchen had a little wood cook stove and boxboard cabinets. The stovepipe was a little too short to reach all the way through the roof, so they had to sit the stove up on bricks to get the stovepipe above the roofline. The inside walls were just the ship-lap boards, no wallpaper or anything on them.

Ag cooked three meals a day, by herself, sometimes for as many as twenty cowboys, depending on how many might be working close by. She never knew, when she started a meal, how many there would be there to eat it. Artie said Ag told him later that the first cake she baked when they were at the feedlot looked so bad that she took it over the hill and threw it away, not wanting him to see it. Artie already knew about it, however. He was riding pasture one day shortly after she threw the cake away and he saw it there in the grass and figured out what must have happened. She really was an excellent cook.

The feedlot work started at sunup and lasted 'til it was too dark to see most days. Artie would get up and get the fire going in the little wood stove, then head out to start the first chores of the day. The steers didn't know Sunday from any other day, so they had to be fed seven days a week. The work was hard, but they were together, and they made it fine that first year.

The year before Artie and Ag moved to the feed pens, all the corn was hand chopped and fed to the steers. At the start of the feeding season in 1937, Daubes bought a little Farmall '20' tractor and a "swinging hammer feed mill" to save having to chop all the corn with a hand axe. That thing could really chop the corn. They would stick the corn into the hopper, stalks and all, and it would come out about the consistency of ground feed. It sure took a lot of the work out of preparing the feed for the steers on a daily basis. That old mill is sitting beside the windmill at the West Ranch today.

When the steers would get on their feed good and putting on the weight, they would get pretty buggery. They were used to the feed pen hands and the way they moved around, so wouldn't pay much attention to them. If someone they didn't know came around, they were likely to run. The hands had a set way of moving around the pens. They would enter the pens at a certain place every time and leave the pens in a certain place. If the steers saw anyone coming into the pens from a different direction, they would run. They always kept a good gentle horse up by the house twenty four hours a day. If something spooked the steers, somebody would throw a rope or a hackamore on the horse and head down to the pens as fast as they could get there. They would go to hollering at the steers and the familiar voice would settle them down. Somebody had to be there at all times to keep the steers calm in case something happened. That chore fell to Artie and Ag on Saturday night since the boys all wanted to go to town and maybe to the show.

Mr. Daube would come over at times just to check on the steers. He would open the gate and drive down to the pens in his car just to look the steers over. Dave Daube was the manager of the Daube's Department Store in Ardmore, but he would come over to the feed pens occasionally to see the steers. He was Leon Daube's brother. Dave was likely to stop at the gate and about run his battery down honking for somebody to come and open the gate for him.

One day Mr. Daube and Tom Cardwell were over at the feed pens just looking the steers over and they were counting steers in a certain pen. Tom Cardwell was as good as they came at counting cattle, but Mr. Daube was counting as well and he had a habit of calling out the numbers as he counted. Every time he did that, it would mess Tom's count up and he would have to start over counting. Finally, after about the third time of starting over, Tom had all he could take of that. "Mr. Daube," he said, "you get way over there by that gate and don't you come back over here 'til I get through counting these steers."

Another time though, Tom Cardwell was over checking on the steers. He and Artie were just standing there visiting and looking the steers over.

"How many steers you got in that pen Artie?" Tom wanted to know.

"There's a hundred and one head in there," Artie replied.

Tom counted the steers again. "I don't believe there is but a hundred head in that pen," he said.

"Nope, there's a hundred and one head, " Artie said.

Tom counted them for the third time. "You know, you're right," he said. "When you think you're right, don't ever let anyone make you believe you're wrong."

Orb Bulman would deliver propane to the ranch and he loved to look at the steers when he would come by. He told Artie one day, "Those steers necks are getting shorter every day." It was his way of saying how much weight he thought they were putting on.

When the season at the feedlot was wrapping up around the end of January 1938, they didn't know if they would have a job or not. After all, they had been hired to run the feedlot and the feedlot was empty, at least until the following fall. They were milking three or four old cows at the time and when they would get through milking they would take the milk up to the house. Jude would usually come on up to the house and he would give out the work orders for the day. Jude was a quiet man and would often just sit at the table with his head down, lost in his thoughts. One morning they were sitting around the table, Artie, Richard Pitmon, Duter Conner, and Jude. Jude was sitting there with his head down, not saying anything. The others were sitting there waiting on their orders for the day. Duter was quite a comedian and when Jude finally raised his head and looked up, Duter said "How dee do." Jude couldn't help it; he had to laugh.

Jude and Otherine Kingsberry had a boy named Wilson and he was quite a handful. Artie would babysit Wilson while he went about his work a lot of the time. One morning they were sitting at the table getting ready to start the day. Jude finally looked up and started giving out the work orders. "Richard, you and Duter hitch up the wagon and get started feeding," he said. Artie you take Wilson and patch a little on the feed pen fence if you get a chance. Main thing though, just watch Wilson. He figured that would be a full time job more or less.

The feedlot was located at the far northeast corner of the East Ranch, about four miles north of the Pennington Creek bridge. A man by the name of James Hutchins was working on the ranch and lived in the little house west of the corrals over by the main ranch house. He was being moved down to the Sheep Ranch and Artie and Ag moved into the house he had been living in around the first of February 1938. It was a little three room house and Daubes bought them a roll of wallpaper to put up to make it look a little more like home. Ag went to Ardmore and bought $106 worth of furniture. She got a couch, a bed, a dinette set, even linoleum for the floors. They told her at the furniture store, if they didn't have to deliver the furniture, they would throw in a pretty little table she had been admiring. Duter Conner used one of Daube's trucks and hauled it home for them. That little table sits today in a prominent place by the window in Artie's living room.

Ag started working for the election board in 1938 and served on that board for more than 38 years. There were over 500 people vote in the 1938 County election in Mill Creek alone. That number did not include the folks that voted in Frisco and Troy. The woods were full of people at that time.

They stayed in the little house until the tragic accident at the Rock Wool Plant south of Mill Creek in May 1938. Jude Kingsberry met Mr. Cardwell at Tishomingo and they went to a Cattlemen's Association meeting. When the meeting was over, Tom Cardwell headed back to Ardmore and Jude started home to the ranch northeast of Mill Creek. The weather had turned stormy and the wind was blowing something fierce by the time Jude got to Troy. At that time, old highway 22 crossed the railroad tracks near Troy Oklahoma. Jude never saw or heard the train that hit him. They called the train that killed Jude Kingsberry, "Black Gold" and it was a fast moving train that made few stops. The car was rolled up and smashed so badly by the collision that it was unrecognizable. They held the funeral in the ranch house where he lived with his wife Otherine. With the damage to the car, one would have thought the body would have been badly disfigured, but when the casket was opened, a dark bruise on Jude's cheek was the only visible evidence he had been in the wreck. Jude started working for the Daube family in 1921 and was killed in May 1938. He drove a 1926 Model "T" roadster.

Otherine was so shaken and distraught by what had happened to her husband, she asked Ag and Artie to stay with her in the main ranch house until she felt she could cope with the loss. Her son Wilson was four years old at the time. He thought a lot of Artie and would follow him around while he went about his work. ***(Author's note: Many years later, after Artie had retired, Wilson put on a dinner for Artie, Arvel Pitmon, and J.W. Standifer)***. They moved up to the ranch house the day after the funeral and would stay there with Otherine until August of that year. Wilson would go in the wagon with Artie to feed and he could never understand why the windmill wouldn't turn every time he wanted a drink. Wilson was only four years old but had a mature mind for his age. Not long after Artie and Ag moved into the ranch house with Wilson and Otherine, they had just gone to bed one night when Wilson came into the bedroom.

"Artie," he said quietly. "You know what we need to do?"

"What's that Wilson?" Artie replied.

"We need to move them sheep back over here. That's what my daddy would want us to do." They had sheared several head of sheep and moved them to the east side of the ranch before Jude got killed. Wilson knew the sheep needed to be brought back home.

At the end of August, they moved back to the feed pens, and were glad to get back to living by themselves again. The ranch house had become like Grand Central Station compared to what they were used to with people coming and going all the time.

When they moved back to the feed pens, Mr. Cardwell told Ag to take whatever she needed from the little house on the ranch that they had lived in for a while. She took the stove, remembering the little stove she started out with there and how inadequate it was. They also took the linoleum to put down on the boxboard floors. Before they moved in, they took out one of the partition walls and made the room where they stayed twice as big as it was. It was now a rather large 10 foot by 20 foot room. The other ten foot by ten foot room served as the kitchen. They put beaver board up on the inside walls and linoleum on the floors. Made a pretty good looking little house out of it.

Leroy Pitmon was staying at the feed pens most of the time, so they built a little room on the side of the house for him to sleep in. The walls were of 12 inch planks just butted up together. When it snowed, the snow would blow in between the planks and onto the bed.

Everett (Mutt) Garrison was a frequent visitor to the feed pens. He would come for a visit and just stay several days at a time. You never knew when he was going to show up, how long he was apt to stay, or when he was likely to leave. Ag would look out the door and say," here comes Mutt, no there goes Mutt." Mutt was a real horseman. He could do anything to a horse or on a horse that needed to be done.

The feed pens that year were full of three year old steers. Those 400 head of steers could really put away the feed. They had a daily ration of 29 pounds each that consisted of 24 pounds of corn (Shuck, cob, and all ground up together), 4 pounds of cotton seed cake, and one pound of sweet feed. The steers got fed four times a day. They also fed around 30 bales of prairie hay a day. As the steers would fatten up, they would require less and less hay, getting most of the roughage they needed from the corn. By the time they were ready for market, the four hundred head of steers would only be eating around four bales of hay a day.

The first feeding was at 6:00 o'clock in the morning, then at 10:00 o'clock. The afternoon feedings were at 2:00 o'clock and 4:00 o'clock. Then they had to get the first morning feeding ready to go. In between feed times, they would grind and prepare the feed for the next feeding. Chester Belcher, Paul Burk, Mooch Parker, and Artie ground the feed. Mooch was a brother to Tom Parker who was foreman of Gray's Ranch east of Mill Creek for many years. There were also 200 head of hogs to be fed daily.

When the steers were ready for market, they drove them

to the railhead at Mill Creek and loaded them onto boxcars bound for the Chicago Stockyards. There were twelve carloads of steers. The trip took so long, the steers had to be unloaded, watered and fed, two different times before arriving in Chicago. The steers averaged weighing 1348 pounds when they sold at Chicago, and it was estimated that they lost nearly one hundred pounds a head during the trip. They sold for 11.25 cents per pound in the Chicago Stock Yards market.

The next year, Artie did all the feeding and Raymond Howard, Doyle Pitmon, and Dude Conner did the grinding with occasional help from Chester Belcher and Red Akins.

Most years from 1937 to 1942, the feed pen would feed 20,000 bushel of corn a year. The corn prices ran from 40 cents a bushel to 60 cents a bushel depending on what kind of a corn crop there was. That corn came from south of Ardmore, Boggy Bottom around Wapanucka, Paul's Valley, and Wynnewood. It came in wagons and trucks and it took a couple of days to get from Ardmore to the feed pens with a wagon loaded with corn. There were no scales at the feed pens the first couple of years so they would just have to go by the weigh ticket the driver had when he got there with the corn. They would all weigh out when they left wherever it was they loaded the corn. Later on, the feed pens had their own scales and would weigh the corn as it was unloaded.

The corn from up around Paul's Valley came by truck, but most of the old trucks were in pretty bad shape. The tires on several of the trucks were worn out and just barely had a little tread you could see. The corn haulers got five cents a bushel for hauling and they could haul around a hundred bushels at a time. That's five dollars per load. 'Course gasoline was 10 cents a gallon, so five dollars would buy a lot of gasoline. Still, it was pretty poor wages for loading a hundred bushels of corn, hauling it forty or fifty miles to the feed pens, and then unloading it in the sheds.

All the time at the feed pens was not filled with work. There was time occasionally for a little fun, and when the opportunity came along, they usually went about the fun just as hard as they did the work. One day as they were finishing up a day's work, a bulldog wandered onto the place from somewhere and ventured up by the house. They had some "high life" in a bottle and they began to think about how much fun it would be to put a little on the bulldog and see if it would make him leave. They surely didn't want a bulldog hanging around, and they figured the "high life" was about the best way to get rid of him once and for all.

They sprinkled a little of the "high life" on the bulldog's back but he just squirmed a little bit and then went and laid down in the shade. Figuring the stuff must have lost some of its power, they sprinkled a little more on him. Still no response from the bulldog to amount to anything. By that time, they had run out of options. Not knowing how long the "high life" had been lying there on the shelf, they figured it must have just gone bad in the bottle. They finally decided to try one more thing. One of them, ***(Name withheld to protect the guilty)***, took a corncob and ran it back and forth underneath the bulldog's tail a few times then poured on a fair amount of the "high life." That did the trick. That bulldog went to running around in circles as fast as he could run then ran into the feed granary full of shelled corn. He went all the way to the top of the mountain of shelled corn then slid back down on his rump.

Out the door of the granary he went and jumped headlong into a water trough full of water. When the bulldog slid back down the pile of corn, he started an avalanche of corn and most of it ran out the door of the granary onto the ground. It took them 'til almost dark to shovel it all back in. The bulldog, however, was nowhere to be seen. Who would have figured on that?

SHE NEVER DID GET RESTED

It was a Saturday night at the feed pens. The sun was still an hour or so away from going down but all the hands had left for town. The young single guys just couldn't stay hooked at the pens on a Saturday night, so the duty usually fell to Artie and Ag, the old married couple. It had been a fine Indian Summer day, blue sky with a few fluffy white clouds for the sun to hide behind now and then. The steers were lazily feeding from the afternoon ration of ground corn, sweet feed, and cotton seed cake. All was well in the world. Supper was finished, the dishes done and put away, and it was time to just sit, relax, and enjoy what remained of a beautiful afternoon. That is, until the honking of the old truck broke into the otherwise peaceful scene.

As the truck came into view down the road, it was plain

to see it was another load of scrawny old cows Mr. Daube had shipped in from down in Texas. They would be underfed, over mean, and wild as a peach orchard boar most likely. It was a tradition though, for the inevitable load of scrubs to show up just when everything seemed to be going just fine. The cows would have to be put in a separate trap from the steers and would have to have special care to get them by 'til warm weather came along. Still, it was easy to see that they would bring a nice profit in the spring if they could pack some pounds on them through the winter.

Artie and Ag walked down to the pens to meet the truck. There wasn't a loading chute, so as usual, the truck backed down into the low place to unload. When the cows started out of the truck and out into the trap, it was easy to see they were the usual mix of hooves and horns with a little bit of meat and hide in between. If anything, they were even wilder then the cows they usually got each fall.

There was a pretty high piece of ground at the far end of the trap, and the ground went down sharply on the other side of it to a little creek. One of the cows made a beeline for that high piece of ground, and when she went over the top, she lost her footing and went head over heels down the slope to land spraddle-legged on the sandy ground. And there she stayed. Artie tried for a good long while, but he just couldn't get her up.

Meanwhile, the rest of the wild bunch was gathered at the far end of the trap and they looked like a stray tumbleweed or just about anything else would set them to running again. Artie went ahead and put out some feed for them, and before long they began to settle down. The old cow down by the hill, however, was still down.

First thing the next morning, Artie went to check on the down cow. No change as far as he could see. He did take some feed and water down and she managed to eat some and drink a little. Along about noon, Sam Daube showed up.

"What do you think about the cows we sent over yesterday?" He said.

"Well, they're gonna be okay, I guess," Artie replied. "All except one of them, that is."

"What do you mean, one of them?" Sam wanted to know.

"One of them old cows ran off the bluff down at the far end of the trap when we unloaded her. I couldn't get her up last night or this morning either. She did eat a little and took some water though."

"I wouldn't worry much about her," Sam said. "She'll get up when she gets good and rested, I expect."

As the days went by, the cows settled down nicely. They were eating well and even beginning to put on a little bit of weight. The down cow, however, was a different story. They would try every day, but she just wouldn't get up. She was looking poorer and poorer, and Artie knew it wouldn't be long before she was too weak to get up even if she could otherwise. Sure enough, a couple of days later, when he went down to feed her, she was dead. It's just one of the things a cowboy has to deal with. Sooner or later, you're gonna lose a little stock no matter how good a stockman you are.

Artie was down in the feed pen when Mr. Daube opened the gate and drove down to look at the steers. They talked a little while and Mr. Daube commented on how well the steers were doing.

"Say, come to think of it," he said. "How's that old cow doing that was down the last time I was here?"

Artie got that humorous look on his face that we have all seen over the years when he knows he is about to make a point.

"She never did get rested," he said.

MOVE 'EM OUT

To drive 400 head of steers across country was no easy task. To do it with only one cowboy, a kid, and a woman was another matter altogether. That's why the plan was to have the cowboys from the West Ranch meet them at the old public well south of the Bellwood School House. Artie, Ag, and Mutt Garrison would get an early start from the feed pens and ease the steers along slowly. They would meet the other cowboys at noon at the public well.

The country was more or less clear all the way. All they had to do was keep the steers going in a straight line across the prairie. Mutt was on a green broke colt, and would be hard pressed to keep his side straight if there was any unforeseen trouble. Artie had the other side, and with the experienced cow horse he was riding, he didn't figure to have much trouble on his side. Ag was bringing up the rear with her only real responsibility being just to keep them moving and the laggards pushed ahead.

All was going along just fine, and they reached the public well just before noon. They had let the steers take their time, and by the time they arrived, they were content to just graze around or lie down and rest. The three cowpunchers converged on the well and when they had slacked their thirst, they sat around and waited for the help to arrive. The rest of the way to the West Ranch was not going to be so easy. For one thing, they would have to cross the road. With a ten foot gate on either side, it would take a while to get 400 head of steers across. Then after that, Pennington Creek had to be crossed and yet another gate on the other side.

After a wait of about an hour, and with no help in sight, Artie began to think that they might be able to finish the drive themselves. They talked it over and decided they could do it. Besides, they would likely meet up with the other cowboys soon after they got started. Mutt rode down and opened both gates and they started the steers moving toward the road. After the steers started across, Artie and Mutt tied their horses and moved out on foot to keep them going across and not up or down the road. Ag kept them moving from behind.

With all the steers across and going well, Mutt closed both gates and they headed for the crossing on Pennington Creek. The touchy part was negotiating the crossing and getting the steers through the gate on the other side at the same time. It was really slow work, and it took some pretty good riding from all three of them to get it done. Finally, the last steer was through the gate and they all breathed a sigh of relief. The rest of the way was clear going. Just a couple of miles across the prairie to the corrals waiting for them just north of the ranch headquarters.

Mill Creek Stockyards in the early 1940s. Daube steers ready for market.

They got those steers strung out along the creek bottom for a ways and then turned them southwest toward the ranch. There was about a mile of pretty level going, then up the hill and down the other side to the corrals. It took most of an hour, but finally the lead steers crested the hill and started down the other side. They had just been easing them along and taking their time.

Down by the corrals at the ranch the cowboys were saddled up and ready to head over to the public well. Tom Cardwell happened to look up and see the lead steers coming over the top of the hill. He couldn't believe his eyes. How could one cowboy, a kid on a green bronc, and a woman manage to drive 400 head of steers across more than five miles of country, through gates and across creeks by themselves? Of course, what he would learn over the next several years, was that the cowboy in that threesome was not just an ordinary cowboy. He was a cowboy with a natural instinct of how to handle cattle. On more than one occasion over the years, Artie would get more work done with a couple of kids helping him than a lot of folks could get done with three or four cowboys. He became one of the most respected men in the entire country when the talk turned to cattle or horses.

Artie told me one day that he didn't think he taught anybody anything in all his years of working on the ranch. There would be a lot of folks that would beg to differ, I would imagine.

Kenneth Cole's father started in the cattle hauling business in the late 1930's. While helping drive cattle from all over the country to the stockyards either at Mill Creek or Scullin, he saw the need for a better way to get cattle to the railhead. It would take a day and sometimes two to get the cattle from the feedlots or ranches to where they could be loaded onto railcars for shipping to Chicago and other markets. The steers had to be eased along to keep from running weight off of them. There had to be a better way.

Loading steers or other livestock at the railheads at Scullin and Mill Creek was a challenge. They would hitch horses to the empty cattle cars on the siding and pull them onto the track that ran by the loading chutes. When the car was full of cattle, the horses would pull it back onto the siding and spot it for the north bound train to Chicago to pick up. They would continue loading cattle cars until all the steers were loaded and the cars spotted for pickup. This procedure would be repeated at least twice more on the trip to Chicago as the steers had to be unloaded a couple of times for feed and water.

Mr. Cole decided he would buy a truck and trailer and start hauling steers from the feedlots to the railhead. His first truck was a 1936 Chevrolet with a 29 foot bed on it. He could haul about fifteen steers at a time. It took several loads to get all the steers to the railhead, but they arrived in good shape and not stressed. He started hauling cattle for Daubes at the feed lot at Ardmore, then as time went on, he hauled from all the ranches around Mill Creek.

Kenneth started working for his dad hauling cattle when he was only 15 years old in 1946. He hauled cattle to Oklahoma City and the Swift Packing Company in Ft. Worth, Texas. The Daube Cattle Company had a contract with Swift to deliver beef and it saved having to take cattle to the sale barns. The going price for hauling to Ft. Worth was $65 a load. That was a lot of money in those days. He would make three or four trips with about 15 steers on each load. As time went by, he upgraded to a bigger truck and longer trailers. As the years piled up, the Cole Trucking Company became synonymous with livestock hauling in the Mill Creek and surrounding area. Kenneth hauled cattle for 60 years and retired in 2006 at the age of 75.

Today, his son Ronald continues in the business and has a fleet of three tractors and trailers. He hauls mostly long haul loads. Each week, he takes a load of packer cattle from this area to Georgia. After the packers are delivered, he picks up a load of stocker calves and brings them back to the west Texas feedlots and sometimes to feedlots in Nebraska.

Kenneth and Artie have been friends for over sixty years. They worked together to get Daube cattle to market and never had a disagreement in all those years. At least none that either will admit to. Kenneth is quick to heap praise on Artie. "I never had one minute's trouble hauling cattle from Artie's place," he said. "He was always prepared and had the cattle ready to load when I arrived. You won't find a better stockman or a better man." I believe I heard Artie say something very similar about Kenneth, come to think of it.

(Author's note: I thoroughly enjoyed visiting with Mr. Cole and talking about the old days. I phoned over to Connerville to set up an appointment with him one day and his wife answered the phone. In the process of giving me directions to their home, she asked if I knew where the cemetery was in Connerville. I replied that I hadn't been to Connerville in a number of years, but I thought I remembered where the cemetery was back then. I'll never forget her reply. "If you ever knew where the cemetery was, you still do," she said. "They ain't moved it as long as I can remember."

"Yes ma'am," I replied. "I expect you're right. I believe I can find your place." It was one of many humorous moments I ran into while visiting with folks and gathering data for this book.

BROTHERS BY CHOICE, SISTERS BY BLOOD

Artie Quinton and Arvel Pitmon were about as close to brothers as you could get without really being blood brothers. They went to school together at Bellwood as youngsters and took the eighth grade graduation exam together. They both loved to fish and hunt squirrels and they did a lot of both as they grew up in the Bellwood area. As they grew into teenagers, they dated sisters and both eventually married McClure sisters, Agnes and Joanne. They called them Ag and Jo as did most folks. They both became cowboys as a means of livelihood and both eventually became ranch managers. For many years, they lived and worked on adjoining ranches with just a barbed wire fence separating them.

Ag and Jo were as close as sisters could be and they did everything they could together. They would visit back and forth and share the rigors of being a cowboy's wife in the time when there were no conveniences and life was tough living on the ranch. Jo would bundle up the kids and walk the two miles or more across the pasture from the Thompson Ranch to Artie and Ag's house on Daube's East Ranch with a load of clothes wrapped in a sheet and slung across her back. She and Ag would do laundry together. Most generally, Arvel would walk over to the gate that separated the two ranches and help them get across Polecat Creek on the foot log that served as a bridge. Then he would walk back home and get started on the day's work. Sometimes, if the weather was too bad to walk, they would hitch the team to the wagon and make the trip that way. Arvel and Jo had three girls, Wanda, Bonnie, and Arvella.

Arvella was just a little tyke at the time and she was always afraid to cross the foot bridge by herself. Arvel would encourage her to walk across, but most times she would get part way across and just sit down on the log. Arvel would carry her across. On the way back home, Arvel wasn't there to help her across so she would have to do it herself. She would much rather just wade the creek and one day as they approached the bridge, she tried to talk her mother into letting her wade across instead of crossing on the log. Jo told her she thought it was too cold to be wading the creek, but when it became apparent that Arvella wasn't going to cross on the log, she relented and let her wade across. Sure enough, that night she came down with a bad case of the croup and could barely get her breath. Artie and Ag came to check on her and Ag and Jo doused her down with homemade concoctions designed to clear up the congestion. Arvella wasn't sure which was worse, the sickness or the cure.

Not long after the episode with the croup, Arvella took the mumps, but she just had them on one side. Ag went over to check or her but before she got to the house, she hollered and Jo came to the door. Ag was still a pretty fair distance from the house. She asked Jo to take Arvella outside and put her under the tree in the yard so she could come in and talk without getting exposed to the mumps since she hadn't had them. Jo took Arvella out and sat her under the tree like Ag asked her to do, but it didn't stop Ag from catching the mumps. A little while later, Arvella caught them in the other side. Ag wouldn't come to check or her that time.

In or about 1946, the Pitmon family got a car. It was a 1936 Chevy and it made it much easier to take the laundry to Ag's or just to go visit. A lot of the time when Jo would go to visit Artie and Ag, she would go by and pick up Leon McDonald and take him with them. He was just a little boy and Jo enjoyed having him around. When Arvella started to school and her mother kept hauling Leon around with her, it didn't sit too well with Arvella.

The two families would share supper on many occasions. It was just easier to feed both families in that manner than it was to cook two separate meals. Artie and Arvel would meet at a pre-arranged place and time after work and squirrel hunt down the creek until they got a mess of squirrels. They'd take them to whichever household was cooking supper that night and they would have a fried squirrel supper.

Artie, of course, worked on the Daube Ranch and Arvel worked on the adjoining Thompson Ranch for many years. In

1957, Artie moved to the West Ranch and became foreman. But for many years, they worked in close proximity to each other. At roundup time, whether branding and working calves, or shipping cattle to market, the two ranches would help each other get the work done.

Bonnie Jo Pitmon was quite a horsewoman and a good rider. She would ride pasture a lot of the time with Artie and Janet. Arvella wasn't nearly as good a rider but she would ride some with them as well. One day Artie, Janet, and Arvella had been riding pasture and were getting close to home. Arvella was riding a big buckskin horse named Dan that had been raced quite a lot. All of a sudden Janet hollered, "let's race," and away she went with Artie in hot pursuit. Arvella was unable to hold Dan back and after them he went with her struggling to hold on and screaming at the top of her lungs. Artie saw what was happening and started pulling up while hollering for Janet to do the same. Arvella and Dan flew by him like he was standing still and were headed for the gate leading into the home pasture. Problem was, the gate was closed.

Janet saw that Arvella wasn't going to be able to get stopped so she veered over in front of them to try to stop old Dan. Dan swerved to avoid Janet's horse and he slid right into the gate as he was trying hard to stop before he hit it. The sudden stop was more than Arvella could handle. She had barely been holding on as it was, so when Dan stopped so sudden like, over his head she went. She picked herself up off the ground, but her legs were shaking so badly she could barely stand. She refused to ride the rest of the way to the house, choosing instead to walk. She was sure Janet figured all along what was going to happen. I don't believe that for a minute, do you?

Artie Quinton and Arvel Pitmon

Times were rough, especially for women during the period of time up until the late 1940s when at least some modern conveniences became available. Child bearing was an especially difficult event with little to no pain killer available and doctors many miles away. It was not uncommon for both the mother and the child to lose their lives during childbirth as witnessed by the death of Artie's mother and sibling during childbirth. One particular birth experience that was really a miracle was the birth of Arvella Pitmon in February 1941 at the Thompson Ranch house. The story went down like this.

It had been a very wet February and the roads were just

a quagmire. It was an adventure to try to go anywhere with a wagon and team and almost impossible with a car. When Jo Pitmon went into labor, at the house next to the main ranch house, they sent to Mill Creek for old Doc Newberry to come deliver the baby. Doc had all kinds of trouble trying to negotiate the muddy roads to the ranch and when it became apparent that he wasn't going to make it in time, Mrs. Dorothy Thompson sent a rider to fetch Ag. The rider got to Artie and Ag's house just in time for dinner so Ag fed him before she started to the ranch to assist with the delivery. She thought she had plenty of time but as it turned out, she and Doc Newberry would both be too late to help.

Dorothy Thompson was alone with Jo, and with no experience in matters such as this, was forced to deliver the baby. Arvel was there, but was out of his element and was of little assistance. She later said she relied on what she had seen during the movie "Gone with the Wind" and what experience she had with cattle to see her through the ordeal. Bonnie Jo was over at the main ranch house washing dishes and missed the whole thing.

When the baby was delivered into her waiting arms, she could see the umbilical cord was wrapped around the baby's neck and was choking her. In fact, the baby's face was blue and she was not breathing. She spanked the baby soundly as she had seen done, but there was no response. At that point, Arvel went out to the porch, unable to cope with the fact the baby was not breathing. He knew he had to steel himself to tell Jo that her baby was dead. It was about more than he could bear.

Meanwhile, Mrs. Thompson laid the baby in a pan of water she had warmed and began to massage the baby's lungs and body. After what seemed like an eternity, the baby began to cry. She was alive! Arvel rushed back into the house when he heard the cry. When he determined the baby was going to be okay, he went in with tears streaming down his face and told his wife they had a baby girl. Dorothy Mae Thompson saved Arvella's life that day with some help from above. It was just an example of the trials of childbirth in those days. Luckily, this one turned out well. Not all of them did.

Jo McClure Pitmon died a scant eight years later on November 21st 1949 at the age of 35 years. She died of a tubular pregnancy. She had no idea she was pregnant and had been picking up pecans one morning. She and Ag picked up a lot of pecans whenever there was a good pecan crop. Jo had been picking up pecans for a day or two and had two burlap sacks full of pecans, around 200 pounds. She loaded them into the trunk of the car and headed over to her dad's place where they were killing hogs. She hadn't been there long before she got to feeling bad and her dad wanted to take her home but she said she was about to leave anyway so she would be home when the kids got home from school. By the time she got home, she couldn't get out of the car. Her daughters, Bonnie and Wanda, helped her out of the car and into the house. Arvel wanted to take her to the doctor, but she said she wanted her Aunt Eva Garrison to come pray for her. Eva prayed for her and then she told her.

"Jo", she said. "I know we've prayed for you, but I really think you ought to go to the doctor. I just feel like that is what you need to do."

It was late on a Friday afternoon. They took her to the Delay Hospital in Sulphur, Oklahoma. The doctor she would have normally seen was not available. There is some disagreement as to exactly what happened. Jo's daughter Wanda has always maintained that her doctor admitted her, but then left to go to a football game and left her to the care of Doctor Delay. Others remember that her doctor was never there at all.

The short of it, however, is that Doctor Delay was hesitant to do surgery without the approval of her doctor since she was checked in under another doctor's care. When her doctor did arrive on the following Monday morning, he immediately performed the needed surgery. Jo Pitmon died that same night. The last thing Jo said to her girls was for them to be good until she came home to be with them. She never got to go back to her earthly home. Those last words though, have guided the lives of her daughters through the years and helped to mold them into the kind of women of which she would have been very proud.

Artie and Arvel both retired in later years as ranch foremen. They attended the same church for many years, the same church Artie attends today in 2010. Before Arvel's health forced him into a nursing home, the two of them would go to the alter to pray every Sunday at the end of the church service. They remained buddies even in prayer to the God they both worship. Each Sunday when they would finish praying, Artie would tell Arvel, "Here, let me help you up, Old Man." Knowing Artie could barely see, Arvel would return the favor. "Let me help you back to your seat, Old Man," he'd say. It would always bring a smile to both their faces.

A REAL COWBOY

Richard Pitmon was a real cowboy. He was born a few years too late to really fit into the picture we have of the old time cowboys. You know the picture I'm talking about. The old cowboy leaning up against the bar with a drink in his hand. He's got a ten gallon Stetson on his head, a colorful bandana around his neck, plaid shirt stuffed down into a pair of worn slick jeans. The bottom of the jeans stuffed into the twelve inch tops of high heeled cowboy boots. The large rowled spurs twinkling in the light from the kerosene lamp.

He might have been born a generation too late for his persona, but he was just as much a cowboy as the man in the picture. Artie saw him as a father figure. A lot of the things Artie became really good at around cattle and horses, he learned from Richard Pitmon. He is always ready to give credit where credit is due. 'Course a lot of folks get the chance to learn from their predecessors and not all of them recognize the opportunity. You have to have an open mind and be willing to learn. Then too, a little natural ability doesn't hurt either. Artie had both. The will to learn, and the natural ability to excel at what he learned.

Richard was a horse cowboy. From the time he started working for the Daube Ranch in 1922, Richard had a firm belief that anything a cowboy really needed to do on a cattle ranch, he could do horseback. That was the mindset of the old time cowboys that rode for the brand. There was a lot of fence building, pole cutting, and the like going on around the ranch when he first hired on, but if you saw Richard, you saw him on a horse. The other hands did the manual foot work, and Richard did the cowboying.

I was visiting with Artie one afternoon and he got to talking about Richard. He said that during all the years he worked on the ranch he never saw a cowboy that could rope and handle wild cattle out in the pasture like Richard could. They had some pretty wild cattle from down in Texas on the ranch one year and Richard would rope an old cow that needed doctoring and throw her down and doctor her. He was the best at it.

Richard would take an old green broke colt and start riding him. Before you knew it, he would be roping off of that colt. He was a better than fair hand with a rope and would enter steer roping contests around the country. He was always competitive. He was a natural horseman and could teach a young horse how to handle cattle and handle a mean old cow on the end of the rope. He liked things wild and wooly. If he had to rope a cow out in the pasture for some reason and the cow didn't throw a tantrum, he would throw a rope under her or something to get her to show a little fight. He liked to have fun and he liked life with the hair on, as they say. He was the best man on the ranch at counting cattle. He would tie a knot in his bridle reins for every hundred head. He was seldom wrong.

One time Jude Kingsberry took Richard to the Fat Stock Show in Ft. Worth, Texas. When they were in close proximity to the show, they got lost. It was very early in the morning; the sun had not yet risen. They pulled into the driveway of a house that had a light shining and Jude told Richard to go knock on the door and ask which way they needed to go to get to the Fat Stock Show. Richard got out of the truck and went to the door. He had no idea who lived there or anything, but when a man opened the door at his knock, Richard said. ***"You think you can make a living getting up at this time of day?"*** Classic Richard Pitmon.

Of all the good qualities and traits he had, Richard had a bad habit. He just couldn't shake the drinking problem he had. In the later years, Ag Quinton took the time to write down her feelings about a lot of the people she and Artie worked with over the years. Old Sam Daube, Leon Daube, Tom Cardwell, Leo Roberts, and many more. When she got to Richard Pitmon, she only wrote three words. "Whiskey got him". The younger Sam Daube got a kick out of that when he read it.

Richard lived the life of a cowboy to the fullest. He was one of a dying breed when he was living. He would have been in his element driving a herd of longhorns from Texas to Kansas in the 1870s. He worked hard on the ranch for many years. There was no harder worker than Richard. Artie has spoken many times of the fond memories he has of Richard and how he enjoyed working with him. His memory will be synonymous with the Daube Ranch and of how it was when cowboys were really cowboys. He was a colorful part of Artie's life and an integral part of the history of cattle ranching in this area.

Ag always had a mess of chickens. They would usually get a hundred baby chickens at one time. Some of the time, she would have as many as 500 chickens around the place. Ab Howard would usually help when it came chicken plucking time. They would kill thirty-five chickens at a time. It was a tradition to have sardines for lunch on chicken killing day. Ag never could learn to wring a chicken's neck, so she would just step on their head and pull it off. They would heat a big old wash pot full of water to dip the chickens in before pulling the feathers off. The big feathers would be pulled off and the little pin feathers singed off over the fire.

Hog killing time was a big event. It took several folks to kill hogs and the weather had to be cold. They would gather up six or seven men, and Ag and Leota Pitmon would help as well. They would scald the hogs in a vat of boiling water. Artie and Leota would usually render the lard. It took two 20 gallon pots and a 15 gallon pot to do the job. Artie would do the sugar curing and then they would hang the meat in the smokehouse. They would make cracklings and they were a favorite of just about everybody. Lizzie would make souse meat from the hog's head. The hog brains were eaten with scrambled eggs and were a delicacy. Ag and Nellie would fry up some of the sausage, taste it, then add spices until they got it like they wanted it.

The last hog killing at the ranch headquarters didn't turn out too well. Richard Pitmon and Coley Smith were there and were supposed to be helping. The problem was, they had been helping themselves to the 'Who Shot John" a little too much and were dropping the meat in the dirt and everything else. Ag got all she wanted of that and told them both they had better straighten up. Coley asked Richard who that woman thought she was. Richard allowed as how that was Artie's wife and they had better get out of there. He loaded Coley up in the truck and they left.

Ag would always have a garden and canned a lot of both fruit and vegetables. Along with the pork, beef, and chickens, there was always plenty to eat.

They stayed at the feed pens that time for over three years and left on March 20th 1942. Not long after that, a plane crashed about a mile north of Mill Creek. It was a B17 fighter plane. There was only one survivor and he saved himself by parachuting out of the plane before it crashed and landed in a pecan tree. He was from Victoria Texas. Many years later, he came by to visit Artie.

"You remember a plane crash just north of town back in the 1940s," he asked.

"I sure do," Artie replied. "Best I can remember, there was only one survivor."

"I am that man," he said.

Artie and Ag were married eight years before Janet was born. Ag would go with Artie a lot of days just helping him do whatever he was doing on the ranch. They would feed the cattle in the winter with a wagon and a team of mules. One day they loaded the wagon up with bales of hay and took off to feed the cows. The hay was stacked pretty high on the wagon and Ag was riding on top of the hay. They started up a little bank and as the wagon tilted to the side, Artie could see they were going to lose the hay. He was more concerned with Ag's safety then he was the hay.

"Jump Ag," he hollered.

"Just where do you think I'm supposed to jump to?" She hollered back.

The bales of hay started falling, and luckily, some of them fell between the front of the wagon and the mules and landed on the tongue of the wagon. Ag landed on the bales of hay and was saved from injury except to her pride. Artie decided he had better not stack the hay that high on the wagon after that incident.

They always had a team of mules in those early years and not all of them were well broken to the wagon. On more than one occasion, they would get spooked over something and Artie would just let them run in a circle until he could get them stopped.

Artie had been working for Daubes about four years and was still making the same $35.00 a month he started out making. He figured it might be time for a raise. It was the only time he ever asked for a raise during the almost fifty years he worked on the ranch.

"Mr. Cardwell," he said. "You reckon I might could get a little raise? I've been working here for a spell now and you know what I've done and what I haven't done."

Mr. Cardwell looked over at him for a minute. "Yea," he said. "I reckon we might do that."

It took three months for the raise to show up on Artie's check. He figured with money being as scarce as it was, they probably had to talk it over a good bit before they gave it to him.

In the 1930's there were three Jewish boys from Ohio that decided they wanted to tour the West. They ended up in Ardmore, Oklahoma and two of the boys decided they would go back to Ohio. The other boy, his name was Abe Sparks, decided to stay in Ardmore. He didn't have a job, of course, and when the police saw him just loitering around town, they called Old Sam Daube.

"Put him up in the Mulkey Hotel," Mr. Daube said. "I'll send somebody over there tomorrow to get him." Sure enough, the next morning, Tom Cardwell picked Abe up at the Mulkey, paid his bill, and took him to the ranch on Rock Prairie. He was a good looking boy, had a head of good looking black hair. Wasn't long before they figured out that head of black hair was full of lice. They took him to Mill Creek to the barber shop and the barber cut his hair and doped his head all up with something to kill the lice.

Abe had never ridden a horse, and they put him on a little brown colt that was green broke. The horse threw him off into a pile of rocks and he hollered for Ab Howard to come and help him. Turns out he wasn't hurt bad, and when he got out of the rock pile, he looked over at Ab with a funny look on his face.

"You know why I was hollering at you?" He asked.

"I don't reckon," Ab replied.

"Well, I landed right on a rock," Abe said.

Ab looked at him with a dour look on his face. "That's the way it always happens son," he said.

They had a lot of fun out of Abe. They even named the little brown horse "Abe" after him. Abe worked for Daubes for a while and ended up marrying a gal from around the Mannsville area. Her maiden name was Dollar. They lived around the Ardmore area for years, and ended up in the scrap iron business on the east side of town. Abe did right well for himself. He never did go back to Ohio, at least not to live. There was a piece in the Ardmore paper about Abe several years back.

One thing that was pretty common among the larger ranches in the 1930s and 1940s was the poor fences. It was common for cattle to drift onto another ranch between roundups. When one of the larger ranches, like Daube's, would get ready to ship cattle, they would call their neighbors to come and cull out the cattle that belonged to them. It was also a common courtesy to help neighbors ship cattle.

The Thompson Ranch would usually "order sell" all their steers to a buyer. Some packing companies preferred to buy cattle via what was called "order buy." It was really a good deal for the seller and the buyer. The packing company knew they had cattle coming and what the price was going to be and the cattle producer was assured of a sale and at a given price. They would have to deliver the steers to Scullin to load them onto rail cars headed for Chicago or some other Location. One particular year, it was really muddy and the trucks loaded with cattle kept getting stuck coming from the ranch to the gravel road. They wasted so much time getting the trucks unstuck that they missed the train at Scullin. They had to wait for the next train and it was daylight the next morning before they got all the steers loaded. Of course the hands from Daubes were all helping out as well, so Artie was in on that just like the Thompson Ranch hands. The Thompson Ranch would return the favor when Daubes started shipping. It was a good opportunity to see the hands from the other ranches, and they usually made a celebration out of it with a cookout when the work was done.

One fall day as the Daube Ranch was getting ready to round up cattle for shipping on all the ranches, Tom Cardwell, Harmon Clark, and Richard Pitmon were at Artie's place on the East Ranch and got the opportunity to see one of the great bronc rides in the history of the Daube Ranches. Ole Hawk was a raw four year old that had been brought in to break. He had thrown several cowboys and had yet to be ridden. For some reason, Artie picked that morning to give him a try. What resulted was a classic battle between horse and man. Artie rode Hawk to a standstill that morning and the ride inspired Tom Cardwell to make the following statement to the rest of the cowboys later on that day.

"I watched a cowboy make the best ride on a bronc this morning that I've ever seen. I'll tell you all right now, none of you are even good enough to sit on the rail fence and watch him ride."

OLE HAWK

He stood with his back to the split pole corral
Ole Hawk was watching him that he could tell
For now things are peaceful but that wouldn't last
His destiny calls and the die has been cast

For Hawk was a bucker as everyone knew
They lined up to try him the number not few
The best of the cowboys they all took their turn
But the dust of the horse pen is all they did earn

The loop went out smoothly from the cowboy's hand
Like the strike of a snake from the smooth desert sand
Round the neck of the outlaw as light as a kiss
From a pretty young cowgirl a fair country Miss

His hand on the neck like the touch of a lover
The chance was there now might not be another
His foot found the iron to the seat he did leap
His hand gripped the reins as he settled in deep

Ole Hawk stood there quietly a second or two
With a snort of defiance to the heavens he flew
He came down stiff legged his hooves hit the ground
But the cowboy upon him was still there he found

The dust from the ground rose up to the air
The cowboy rode bravely not even a care
His hat pulled down tightly up there on his head
The look on his face like one from the dead

Bucking and spinning the battle began
Hawk tried all his tricks then tried them again
But the cowboy hung grimly there in his seat
It was time for Ole Hawk to finally be beat

Sweat turned to foam on the skin of the beast
But the cowboy kept riding not caring the least
Ole Hawk was a tiring, his head hung down low
He kept on a bucking but was starting to slow

With one final leap he reached for the sky
If this didn't work it would be his last try
He'd run out his string in the horse pen that day
The cowboy upon him would soon have his way

With a snort of disgust he raised up his head
The day was upon him the day he did dread
For the cowboy sat still in his leather abode
Tell all the cowboys, Ole Hawk has been rode

Ted L. Pittman

The first car Artie ever owned was a worn out Pontiac. Ag said they pushed it more than they rode in it. He bought it from a Chevrolet dealer at Sulphur by the name of Brewer. The old car was on its last legs and the tires were worn out as well. Artie didn't know anything about a car, and it was evident he got a bad deal. He even forgot to get his gas stamps that went with the car, and when he got to Mill Creek, he went to Mr. Young's station to get a little gas.

"Where are your gas stamps?" Mr. Young asked him.

"I don't have any gas stamps," Artie replied.

"Well, I guess I'll let you have the gas and you bring me the stamps."

Artie got the four gallon gas allotment he was entitled to and drove the car home. You were only able to get gas stamps that would allow you to purchase four gallons of gas a week because of the war.

One day as Artie was riding in from the pasture, he noticed a lot of car tracks in the yard. He couldn't imagine what had happened. Ag came out of the house and was ready to go to town. Chester Belcher had delivered some propane, and she had him pull the old Pontiac with the propane truck to get it started. Then she just left it running until Artie got home. He rushed to unsaddle the horse and away they went to town while they had a chance.

The Howard children all received a piece of the old home place. Artie got his momma's part and so had twenty acres.

Tom Cardwell had asked Artie if he wanted to sell the twenty acres he had gotten of the Howard place since all the other Howard kids were selling their part to him. He told him he would when all the others had sold theirs. Daubes agreed to have separate abstracts and deeds made up so all the Howard kids could sell their twenty acres individually to them.

Ab was the first to sell, and he sold his twenty acres to Daubes for $15 an acre. A total of $300.00. Then he told Tom Cardwell he wanted a Stetson hat to boot from the Daube store, so Tom gave him one. Edith Howard wanted a new dress, so when she and Raymond sold their twenty acres to Daubes, they got $300 and a new dress. Cecil had sold his land just before Raymond, and when he heard about the dress, he went to Daube's Department Store in Ardmore and told them he wanted a dress too, so they gave him one.

In 1942,there was an eighty acre parcel of land for sale just across the road south from Horace Cook's place. Peirce told Artie he would take forty acres of it if Artie wanted the other forty. The price was $9 per acre. Artie and Ag were still at the feed pens at the time, but had managed to put back a little money and they decided to buy the forty acres. They took the $300.00 they got from Daubes for the 20 acres and put $60 with it and bought the forty acre plot. They bought a three room house at Fittstown for $190.00 and it cost $22.50 to have it moved. Arvel and Jo Pitmon lived in that house for a while.

There was a man from Ardmore cleaning out a well on Peirce's place and Artie asked him what he would charge to dig a well on his place. The going rate was a dollar a foot, but the man agreed to drill the well for seventy-five cents a foot since he was already there. They hired Bill Wright to build a porch onto the house and underpin it. Later, they built a log barn and a shed. Pierce and Ott McDonald put siding on the outside walls. It was fixed up pretty nice. Artie and Ag never lived in that house.

In 1948, the old Pontiac Artie had bought just wasn't going to go anymore, so when Leon Daube asked them if they wanted to buy his wife's car they decided they would. In June 1948, they bought the 1946 Oldsmobile from Leon Daube for $1,250. It had 16,068 miles on it. It was a real luxury after the adventures with the Pontiac. They sold the house and forty acres to Ott McDonald for $1500, of course $1250 of it went to pay for the Oldsmobile. They were sure proud of that car. It would start every time they got in it to go to church or somewhere and was a far cry from what they had been used to. Not long after they bought the Oldsmobile, a bazaar series of events happened involving that car as you will see in later chapters.

PART SIX: HOME ON THE RANGE 1945-1975

A big change came for the Quinton family on March 24th, 1945. A daughter was born and they named her Janet. Artie fell in love with the cute little girl the first time he saw her. Her smile would just melt his heart. He started taking her with him horseback all over the ranch before she could walk. He would take a few cookies and some water along, and, invariably Janet would fall asleep and sleep in his arms while he rode pasture.

That winter of 1945 before Janet was born was as bad of a winter as anyone could remember. They calved out 360 heifers over 4,000 acres of pasture that winter. Lost around sixteen or seventeen heifers and had a 66% live calf crop out of them.

By the time she was eight years old, Janet was riding two year old green broke ponies around by herself. The old women would tell Ag that Artie was going to kill that kid, but she was a real cowgirl. The pony she rode most was called "Popcorn" and she would ride many miles following along after her dad. She would always try to get a race started. She loved to race on the horses, even at a young age. Ag lectured them about the dangers of racing around on the horses so they would wait until they got out of sight of the house and then the horse race would begin.

Leroy Pitmon was working on the Sheep Ranch at that time and his son Jackie had a young colt they called "Crackerjacks". In the summer time, when they would ride pasture, Artie would take a salt shaker along and they would go by George Patrick's watermelon patch and get a watermelon to eat. They would sit under a shade tree and feast on the watermelon. Janet and Jackie would ride on the mules when Artie would hitch up the mule wagon to put out cattle salt. Janet and Jackie could both ride very well at a young age and could gather cattle just like the real cowboys. After they moved to the west side of the ranch, Janet would drive the car and Jackie would sit on the fender and shoot Jack rabbits. Don't see many of them around anymore, that may be why.

Top row left to right---Artie and Janet by the corrals—Bonnie Pitmon on white horse, Artie and Janet behind her
Bottom row left to right---Artie, Janet, Ag with 1946 Oldsmobile

MIRACLES ONE RIGHT AFTER ANOTHER

In 1947, miracle of all miracles, running water in the house. Who would have ever thought it? An indoor bathroom a short time later. All from a tank that stood outside and delivered water to the house by gravity feed. 'Course, the water had to be pumped into the tank by means of a gasoline fired pump. A short two years later, electricity would find its way to the Bellwood area. The memory of how it took place is fresh in Artie's mind today.

April 15th 1949. It was a day that the entire Bellwood Community and the surrounding area had been looking forward to for a long time. It was supposed to be "light day". The Rural Electric Cooperative was bringing the miracle of electricity to the rural areas around Bellwood and Mill Creek. With the coming of the electric lines, would be a positive change in the quality of life for the families that called the area home. Just think of the possibilities; electric lights to read by, sew by, or just sit and admire. It would bring about another change that many grew to regret in the coming months and years. It made it easier to stay up later, and therefore harder to get up early. The coming of electricity would be a culture change for many such as hadn't been seen before.

One day in the fall of 1948, Artie was cutting poles south of the Bellwood School House when a man came along and caught his attention.

"Say there, young man," he said. "I reckon I'm lost. Maybe you can help me out. You see, I work for the REA and I'm trying to follow the surveyor's path for the new electric line. I've lost the path, I guess. I can't find the next set of markers. I've got to draw up the path so the pole setters will have something to go by. You seen any flags around here?"

"I believe if you'll just cross Polecat Creek down there, you'll find three or four red flags there on the far bank," Artie replied. "They are there all together. Maybe you can go on from there."

"Thank you kindly," the man said as he headed down to where Polecat Creek was just visible toward the southeast.

"When do you reckon we'll have electricity?" Artie hollered after him.

"Next spring I expect," the man replied. April 15th is the day the lights will come on if things go as expected."

Things went a little better than expected, and the lights came on a day early on April 14th 1949. It was quite a sight. It paved the way for modern farming techniques, such as electric milking machines, grain and feed grinders, refrigeration, and most importantly, lights with the flip of a switch. Before long, there would be television and radio, record players and electric irons. Things were looking up for the Bellwood Community and surrounding areas.

The first thing Ag Quinton did when the lights came on was go to Sulphur and buy an electric iron. It was the first modern convenience she had. They had a propane refrigerator at the time, but replaced it with an electric model shortly after. Glenn Trammel was moving into the ranch house on Rock Prairie, and Daube's put in a brand new electric 'ice box'. It was one of the Sears and Roebuck 'Cold Spot' refrigerators that were popular for many years around that time. One problem though, there was no electricity at Rock Prairie at the time. Mr. Cardwell asked Glenn if he would trade 'ice boxes' with Artie so they would both have a refrigerator that they could use. So they traded and both were happy.

Another of the first things they got was a radio. They would listen to the old radio shows and the music. Ag always loved to dance and they went to a lot of barn dances in the first years of their marriage. Ag loved to dance with her brother John. She danced with Artie a few times, but he would always step all over her feet so she didn't care to dance with him much. Seems like handling a rough bronc or a mean steer was a lot easier for Artie than handling a pretty little lady on the dance floor. Janet would hold onto the drawer knobs on the kitchen cabinets and dance. It kept Artie busy putting the knobs back on the drawers as she pulled them off.

A few years later, in 1956, they got both a telephone and a television. Now they were really uptown. They would watch the "Donna Reed Show", "Dragnet", "Wells Fargo", "The Real McCoys", and "Bonanza."

There was one thing that electricity brought that was an entirely new thing for most folks. The 'light bill'. For many families, it was the first time in their lives that they had a monthly bill to pay. As new electric appliances were added, the 'light bill' would get more expensive. Though folks continued to call it the 'light bill' for many years, the real costs were associated with the modern appliances that were added as time went on. Still yet, when the lights went on, it began to get easier to live in rural Oklahoma. Artie an Ag were married 12 years before they experienced this convenience in their own home. I can't imagine the feeling they must have had the first time they flipped the switch and the lights came on.

At the infrequent times that storms or other things cause short delays in electric service today, I am quick to grumble at the outage. You think it's possible we may be just a little spoiled? At times, I grimace when I'm writing the check each month for the 'light bill', but when I think of not having the conveniences associated with electric service, I figure it's well worth the cost. I ***would*** like to have seen Ag's face when the lights came on though.

Starting top left by row--- Ag and Janet by the loading chute on the East Ranch--- Artie and Janet get ready for a snowy ride.
2nd row---Ag and Janet and the 1946 Oldsmobile-- Janet rides a bull (notice Artie is not quite hidden behind the bull)
3rd row---Cowgirl Janet with her dog-- Janet rides a pig

A THIEF IN THE NIGHT

It was in October 1948 and it was on a Sunday night. Artie and Ag had started home from church in the 1946 Oldsmobile they had recently purchased from Leon Daube. They got about a block from the church and the thing just quit running. Artie, not being much of a mechanic, raised the hood to see if he could see what the problem might be. He noticed right off that there was a wire hanging down that didn't look like it ought to be hanging there. He grabbed the end of it and it looked like it might be the distributor wire. Sure enough, he stuck it back into the distributor and the car started right up. They got home without any more trouble and he parked the Oldsmobile under the little carport in front of the house. Before long, it was time for working folks to be getting some rest so they got ready and went to bed.

Artie was having some trouble getting to sleep and around 2:00 o'clock, he thought he heard a noise. He eased out of bed and opened the bedroom door and stepped out on the step. He noticed right off that the car was sitting there with the motor running. About that time, the car started backing out of the carport and had the lights on bright. He could see somebody sitting in the driver's seat so he hollered at him to stop a couple of times. The car just kept on backing out real slow like the guy didn't really know how to drive. Artie had taken a gun outside with him and it was loaded. By that time, the guy had opened the car door and when the dome light came on, Artie could see it was a man and he was bare headed. About that time, the man jumped out of the car and took off running. He sounded like a horse running he was running so fast. Artie hollered for him to stop and shot over his head a couple of times but he just hit another gear and was gone.

Meanwhile, the car was just sitting there running, but it looked like someone was sitting in the back seat by the window. Artie was a little bit afraid to head out that way, not knowing who was in the car or if they might have a gun or something, so he decided to wait him out for a while. He sat up the rest of the night waiting on the other man in the car to make a move but he never did. When it got daylight, he could see that what he thought was another man in the car was really his own coat hanging on a hanger in the back seat.

By that time it was getting onto time to start feeding so he saddled up a horse. Leroy Pitmon lived a mile and a half west of where Artie lived on the East Ranch and was helping feed at the time. The first thing he noticed when he got there was the car sitting there with the door open.

"What you fixin to do Artie?' He asked.

"Somebody tried to steal my car last night and I'm fixin to go see if I can find him."

"I run into a boy over by the Bray Bridge just a few minutes ago'" Leroy said.

"Was he bare headed?" Artie wanted to know.

"Yea, he was bare headed and was wet clear up to his knees," Leroy responded.

"Well, I'm going after him," Artie said. He got on his horse and took off down the road toward the Bray Bridge. Wasn't long 'til he run onto Richard Pitmon in his truck.

"Where you headed in such a hurry?" Richard hollered.

"Somebody tried to steal my car last night and Leroy said he saw a boy over by the Bray Bridge. I want to talk to that boy. He ought to be over about Roy Quinton's place by now."

"Tie your horse up somewhere and get in," Richard said. "We'll drive around there and see if we can find him."

They finally caught up with him between Horace Cook's place and the Pennington Creek Bridge. "Let me talk to him," Artie said, and when they pulled close he got out of the truck and walked over to where the kid had stopped on the side of the road. He was just a kid, looked to be fourteen or fifteen years old. You've got to understand now, this was just shortly before Artie got saved and he still had a little bit of that Quinton temper that would find a way out of him on occasion.

"Where was you about 2:00 o'clock this morning?" He asked.

The kid couldn't talk, and probably couldn't hear, but Artie didn't know it at the time. The kid never said a word.

"I'll tell you where you was," Artie said. "You was over at my place trying to steal my car, that's where you was."

About that time, he begin to worry that the kid might have a gun in his pocket so he told him to turn his pockets inside out. The kid finally understood what he wanted him to do, and when he turned his pockets inside out all he had was a broken pencil stub.

They finally decided they would take him to Sulphur, so they loaded him in the truck between 'em so he wouldn't try to jump out or anything. When they got to Sulphur, they stopped at Marvin Burks DX Station there on the corner of Oklahoma Street and Highway 177. ***(Authors note: Today there* is *a Snack Shak store where the DX Station was located in 1948.)***

By that time, they had figured out the kid was deaf, so Richard called the superintendent over at the Deaf School and he came down to the station. He recognized the kid right away and said they thought the kid had gone home. He said the kid stayed at the school part of the time and at home part of the time. His father was a street sweeper for the city but was presently over in the western part of the state pulling bolls. He offered to call him and ask him to come home, but Artie didn't want him to have to go to that much trouble. They finally decided to take him over to the courthouse.

Lynn Norman was Prosecuting Attorney at the time and so they asked for him when they got to the courthouse. Artie explained what had transpired up to that point and asked Mr. Norman what he thought they might do with the kid.

"Been me, I'd of shot him," Mr. Norman said.

"Why no, I wasn't going to shoot him," Artie replied. "I sure don't want to hurt anybody."

"Well, he'd of been paid for," Lynn replied.

"I don't care if he would have been paid for, I don't want to kill anybody," Artie said. "If you don't do something with him though, somebody is sure enough liable to shoot him."

"Well, we've got some pretty rough customers in the County Jail," Lynn said. "I don't think it would be a good idea to put him in there with them. Let me see if I can round up a judge and get some advice on what to do with him. In a couple of minutes, the judge showed up, and after talking a little while it was decided they would put him in solitary confinement and put him on nothing but light bread and whole milk for three days.

The kid was only fourteen years old as it turned out, and Artie took an interest in his welfare. He decided he would keep track on what was happening with the kid and see what he made of his self. He checked on him occasionally and one time when he went to check on him, the kid was just getting over an appendix operation. On one of the occasions he went to visit he asked the superintendent a question that had been bothering him since the night of the car heist. The kid had left the school on a Friday night and it was Monday morning when they caught up with him. What had the kid been eating all that time? The superintendent asked him and he said he hadn't eaten anything except persimmons.

The last time he went to check on him, they told him the kid was gone. He had developed such a bad temper that they couldn't do anything with him so they had to send him to some kind of institution. He sure was a strange kid, and turned out pretty bad. Artie never heard of him again.

In the late 1950s, they hired an old kid on the East Ranch who claimed to be from St. Louis. When he hired on, he gave his name as Joe Miller. He was just a kid, not much more than sixteen years old. He professed to be a cowboy and needed a job working on a ranch. He was a funny kid. He would roam around the ranch at night with a flashlight and catch frogs at some of the stock tanks. One time, he put some of the frogs in Ag's laundry basket with the clothes and that didn't set well with her at all. One morning not long after he hired on, Joe and Artie were at the corrals one morning getting ready to do some riding. Artie pointed out what horse Joe was to ride and went on about saddling his own horse. When he happened to look aver at Joe, he had the bit in both hands trying to stick it in the horse's mouth.

"I don't believe you've ever even rode a horse Joe," Artie told him.

"Well, I have," Joe replied.

"Where did you ever ride a horse before?" Artie wanted to know.

"I rode around a brush fence one time up in Arkansas," he said.

"Where did you go to school?" Artie asked.

"I went to school in Arkansas," Joe replied.

"What were some of your teachers' names boy?"

"I never had but one teacher and we just called her "Old Crow," Joe said. Artie just kept on asking questions just to see how much the kid would lie and there didn't appear to be an end to what he would lie about.

It was plain to see that this kid would tell a lie when the

truth was easier. Ag was just really scared of the kid and it was apparent he wasn't gonna work out, so Artie told Richard Pitmon to tell Tom Cardwell that he wanted him to come and get him.

Meanwhile, Joe told Artie that he wanted to go to work on a horse ranch. He had the Wagner Horse Ranch in mind. Joe was making $15 a month at the time and Artie told him he would pay him an extra month's pay if he wanted to go ahead and leave. Pretty soon Tom Cardwell came to the ranch and picked Joe up. He told Artie later that he hadn't even gotten to where the road turned west at Gray Ranch before he knew that Joe had problems. He didn't last any time at the Wagner Horse Ranch and Artie lost track of what happened to him.

In the 1970s Joe stopped by to visit with Artie and Ag just out of the blue one day. He was married and had his wife with him. He asked Ag if she remembered him and she said, "Now how do you think I could ever forget you?" Turns out his name wasn't Joe Miller at all, it was Nolan Ramsey. He had lied about that as well. He left that day and was never heard from again by anyone on the ranch. I doubt very seriously that anyone ever lost any sleep over that.

SAVED, AND DOING GOD'S WORK

"There is nobody who has reached the age of accountability, the Bible says, that hasn't felt the Holy Spirit."

We were just sitting and visiting and Artie shared that thought with me. "I was just riding the pastures by myself," he said. "Riding pasture gives a fellar a lot of time to think. The Lord was working on me and I was a miserable man. I knew I was going to have to do something. I finally told the Lord if he would let me get to church on Sunday, I'd either get saved Sunday morning or Sunday night. Ain't it strange how folks will set a timetable for the Lord that suits them?"

At that time, there was a pretty good crowd at the church most every Sunday morning and Sunday night. Some nights, there would be about as many people outside as there was inside. There was a lot of fellowship back then. There was a preacher there from Tishomingo named Brother Brooks. He carried a little day book with him all the time.

"I can preach any sermon on any subject at any time," he was fond of saying. "I've got all the subjects and the verses that go with them right here in this day book." Well, Artie really liked Brother Brooks and he sat and listened to the sermon that morning. When the alter call came, nobody made a move and neither did Artie. Finally, Brother Brooks just stepped off the little stage made of two by fours. "Is there anyone here who would like for me to put them on my prayer list?" He asked.

Artie raised his hand, but not very high. It was, however, high enough for John Brock to see it and he headed that way.

"You ready to go to the alter Artie?" He asked. Artie just shook his head in the negative.

"Do you mind if I pray for you?" Brother Brock asked.

"No, I don't mind," Artie managed to get out.

Brother Brock began to pray, and the more he prayed, the more miserable Artie felt. Brother Brock began to pray louder, and the louder he prayed, the more the sweat ran down Artie's face. Finally, he had all he could take. The Holy Spirit had him under conviction, Brother Brock was praying, Brother Brooks was praying, and folks were shouting "Amen."

"I'm ready to go," he finally said. Brother Brock just kept on praying.

"I'm ready to go to the alter," he repeated a little louder. When that didn't get Brother Brock's attention, he just pushed down on John's shoulder and hollered, "I'm ready to go." With that, he just got up and started pushing his way past the preacher and down the pew to the aisle.

By that time, he was so ready to get to the alter, that he

forgot and went to the alter where the women prayed. It didn't matter though. When he finished praying, folks asked him if he got saved. Artie is a firm believer that you have to possess what you profess, so he wanted to make sure he was saved before he proclaimed it to the world. Before he got home that morning though, the lord just flooded him with the Holy Spirit and he knew he was indeed saved. It was the Sunday before Thanksgiving 1948. He has been in church ever since.

Ag was saved a couple of years before Artie, and she told him there were three things she wanted to do. Have family prayer, ask God to bless their food, and pay tithes. They did all three for more than fifty years.

One of Artie's favorite scriptures is Matthew 11: 28-30. ***"Come unto me, all ye that labour and are heavy laden and I will give you rest. Take my yoke upon ye and learn of me, for I am meek and lonely in heart and ye shall find rest unto your souls. For my yoke is easy and my burden is light."*** Artie has passed on the plan of salvation to a lot of folks over the years.

The Holy Ghost was working on Lloyd (Sot) McDonald and he wanted to get saved. Artie, and some others as well, would go down and pray with him but he just couldn't get saved. He was honest about it and he said he just knew he wasn't saved. Finally, one night he dreamed he was at the Church Of Christ and got saved. Somebody told him they thought that he ought to go to the Church Of Christ since he dreamed about it. The next Sunday, he went and sure enough he got saved and his brother baptized him. There is no substitute for determination and being where the Lord wants you to be.

Artie taught the Bible Class at church for thirty-eight and a half years, teenagers for three years, and the juniors for one year. He was Youth Director for thirteen years and on the Deacon Board for forty-nine years. The first Deacon Board was in 1951 and the members were Claude Gaddis, Artie, and Horace Cook. The only regular attendees at church from the old guard these days are Artie, and Horace and Hazel Cook. Arvel Pitmon is in a nursing facility and is unable to attend. He was a corner post of the church for many years, and the church misses his guidance and leadership.

The first baccalaureate service that Artie was on was in 1959. It was the year Arvella Pitmon graduated. Lloyd Harden was Superintendent of the school at that time.

Artie has been pallbearer for a lot of funerals, and later God showed him he would also help with a lot of funerals. The first funeral he helped with was in 1958 and it was the funeral of Mrs. Dowdy. The funeral was at Madill and the weather was terrible. The preacher was old and not feeling well, so Bill Dowdy asked Artie if he would do the graveside service and the closing, so he did. It was the start of a long standing service of assisting and conducting funerals for him. Artie has either assisted or conducted seventy-seven funerals over the years. More than most preachers, I would dare to say. Thirty-nine of them are buried in the Mill Creek Cemetery. Others were strung out in places such as Elmore City, Tishomingo, Troy, Ada, Ardmore, Sulphur, Drake, Russett, Mannsville, Condon Grove, Dickson, Connerville, Dougherty, and the Browning Cemetery. He even conducted one in Kansas. He helped with the funeral of Ruby Clark. She was his sister, and he considered it a privilege to assist.

Graves were hand dug for the most part in those days. Men from the community would gather at the cemetery and spend the day digging the grave. J.T. Clement would usually furnish sandwiches and drinks. There would always be a few loafers in attendance as well. They didn't do much digging, but they could sure put the sandwiches away. Finally, it was approved so the County Commissioners could use county equipment and manpower to dig graves. It sure saved a lot of time and work.

Top row left to right---Ag gets ready to ride, Artie and Ag in 1960
Bottom row left to right—Artie and Ag, date unknown, Artie, Artie

COWBOY LIFE IN THE EARLY 1950S

Don Payne was raised in the Concrete area south of Mill Creek. They had church at the Concrete School House and Don's mother would pack up the kids and off to church they'd go. In the late 1940s, they started going to church in Mill Creek. At the time, church was held in one of the buildings on Main Street. That is when Don first met Artie Quinton. It would turn out to be a good association and in the early 1950s, Don went to work on the ranch with Artie. He was just one of the boys and young men that would work for Artie over the years and live in the little bunkhouse between the main house and the corrals on the East Ranch.

Don would sleep in the bunkhouse, but took all his meals in the main house with Artie, Ag, and Janet. He would take baths in the house and Ag would do his laundry just like she did Artie's. Being with the Quinton family was just like being at home. They treated him just like one of the family and he looked on them as a second mother and father. Janet was like a little sister to Don and he called her "The Little Pest."

Janet rode the bus to school from the East Ranch when she got old enough to attend. John McDonald was the bus driver. ***(Author's note: Not the same John McDonald who was a brother to Ott McDonald.)*** Ag always had a few pigs around the place and one morning John ran over one of them with the bus and killed it. Of course he didn't mean to do it, but it still didn't set too well with Ag. A few days later, the bus let Janet off at the house and John started off then came to a stop and just sat there in the bus. Janet rode her bike down to where he was stopped. "What did you do John, run over another pig?" She asked. She wanted to make sure he didn't forget about it.

During the two years he worked on the ranch, Don got a lot of opportunity to talk to Artie as they rode pasture, fixed fence, or whatever else needed doing. Mostly Artie talked and Don would listen. They would work seven days a week most of the time, except they would knock off in time to go to church on Sunday. A lot of Sundays, Don would ride to church with Artie and Ag, then leave church with his mother to spend the day. That night, he would catch Artie and Ag at church and ride back out to the ranch with them.

Don remembers some of the horses he used to ride. He rode buckskin they called "Dan" and a little horse they called "Popcorn," but his favorite was a little bay horse he called "Shorty." Shorty came from the Rock Prairie Ranch and he had some bad habits when he first came to the East Ranch. If you took the rope off the saddle horn, Shorty would take off running. It took Don a while to break him of that habit. Another of the horses Don liked to ride was a blue roan horse named "Spider."

Artie's favorite horse was a big sorrel horse he called "Flax." Whenever Don saw that Artie was going to saddle Flax, he would always ride Shorty. Shorty wasn't very tall but he was a good fast walker and was the only other horse that might could keep up with Flax across the prairie.

They carried all manner of medicines and such with them as they rode and would doctor cattle as they needed it right out on the open range. There was always a case or two of screwworms that needed to be doctored, and usually it was done just by roping the cow and doctoring her right there in the open. Artie and Don would catch the young bull calves as they were born and work them. The de-horning paste was just starting to be used as well and they would do the de-horning as they worked the calves. One year when it came time to gather and work the calves, Richard Pitmon and Mr. Cardwell were helping. "Why there's nothing left to do," Mr. Cardwell said. "You boys have worked almost everything already."

Sometimes T.J. Patrick would come over to help feed or do whatever they might be doing. One particularly bad winter morning, Artie, Don, and T.J. started out on horseback to feed. At the time, there were feed houses in all the pastures so they would just ride from feed house to feed house putting out feed. Usually the cows would be around the feed house waiting to be fed. If they weren't all there, they would call them up. That morning it was snowing and sleeting so hard you could hardly see your horse's ears in front of you. They started out on the north side in what they called the North Deaver pasture, then swung around and crossed Pennington Creek on the west side into the South Deaver pasture. As they came up out of the creek bottom, there was a fence ahead with a wire gate. T.J. was in front so he hollered out. "I'll get the gate boys." He kicked his horse into a trot and headed for the fence. He was soon out of sight in the swirling snow. Before long, the sound of steeples flying and barbed wire squealing came back to Artie and Don as they made their way slowly out of the creek bottom. They kicked their horses out and got to the fence as fast as they could only to find T. J.'s horse standing there by the fence with his head down. He was twenty or thirty feet north of the gate. As they started to get down from their horses, there came T. J. climbing out of a snow bank. He had missed the gate and hit the fence at a trot. It was a miracle that neither he nor the horse was cut.

"What in the world happened T.J.?" Artie asked.

"Dad gum horse missed the gate," he replied. "I can't figure out why that dumb horse missed the gate."

"Why, that horse couldn't see the gate any better than you could in all this snow and sleet," Artie said.

"Well, he should have known where it was even if he couldn't see it," T. J. said.

Artie just shook his head and got off and opened the gate. Sometimes, it just don't pay to keep a conversation going.

Top left---Artie, Janet, Ag
Bottom left---Artie Janet Ag in 1958
Right---Ag and Artie with the dogs

On one occasion, Artie and Don were riding the South Deaver pasture just checking the cows when they noticed a thunderhead building in the southwest. They didn't think too much about it at the time, but as they cleared the timber where they could see a little better, they could see it was right on top of them. The rain started pouring down, the thunder was loud enough to just about bust their eardrums. The lightning was hitting in the trees and knocked several trees down right close to where they were riding. Don looked down and he could see sparks flying between his horse's ears and from his mane. There wasn't any place to go to get in any kind of shelter so they just rode it out. It was the most scared Don could ever remember being. He just knew any minute he was going to go down to a lightning strike just like the big trees he saw falling everywhere. Someone was looking out for a couple of cowboys that day though and they made it through without incident except for a good soaking.

In the 1950s, most of the feeding was done horseback. At times, if the weather was just so bad they couldn't feed horseback, they would hitch a team of mules up to the wagon and feed that way.

Don remembers making around $35 to $40 a month, of course he got room and board on top of that. Getting to eat Ag's cooking, he figured, was worth about as much as he was making. He would go to Frank Stie's store in Mill Creek on occasion and buy a new pair of Levis. One pay day that he remembered, he bought a pair of Levis and a blue jean jacket. The total came to $7.50.

They always went to church on Sunday and on Wednesday night. One Wednesday night as they were leaving church, T.J. tried to get Artie to ride with him in his new car. At least it was new to him. It was a 1939 Ford. It was shiny black and the prettiest little car you ever saw.

"Come on and ride home with me Artie," he said.

"Naw, I think I'd better drive my own car home," Artie replied. "You go ahead and we'll follow you."

T.J. took out of there at a high rate of speed, and before long was clean out of sight. There was a sandy spot in the road just before the curve at the Pennington Creek bridge and when T.J. hit the sand, he rolled the little Ford. It was in the wintertime and the temperature was in the twenties. The car was lying on its side in the bar ditch, and T.J. decided he'd just stay in the car 'til Artie came along. Before long, he could hear the gasoline gurgling in the tank and fearing the car might catch on fire, he climbed out the window and was standing on the road when Artie, Ag, and Don drove up.

"You okay T.J.?" Artie asked.

"Yea, I'm okay, but I'm cold," T. J. replied with his teeth chattering. "I knew you'd be along in a little while."

They managed to roll the car back up on its wheels and it started right up. T. J. took off, but this time he was going a lot slower as he rounded the curve and went over the Pennington Creek Bridge.

They were working cattle on the West Ranch and Don and Artie went over to help. J.B. Johnston and Finis Clement were working for Richard Pitmon on the West Ranch at the time. ***(Author's note: J.B. Johnston was my uncle by marriage and was married to my Aunt Jean, my mother's sister).*** They were saddling up some horses in front of the saddle shed when Artie and Don rode up.

"I think I'll ride that old colt I've been working out," J.B. said.

"You might want to ride something you can depend on a little more," Richard replied.

"Aw, I think he'll be okay," J.B. said.

He got the colt saddled and just as his rear hit the saddle, the horse just turned and ran in under the shed that ran west from the saddle shed. That shed was at least a hundred feet long and was a lean-to type of a shed. When he got up under the shed, that colt went to bucking and headed down the shed bucking every jump. J.B.s head was banging into the sheet iron top of the shed at every jump, but somehow he managed to duck all the two by four rafters along the way. He finally managed to get the colt shut down about half way down the length of the shed. He rode back up to where they were all standing beside the saddle shed.

"Alright, let's go," he said.

Don stood on the fence so he could see onto the top of the shed and he could see humps in the sheet iron where J.B.s head had hit between every rafter.

Finis Clement always rode a big old paint horse. He thought that horse was the best cow horse there ever was. He would never get faster than a slow lope. One day they were gathering some cows and Finis kicked the old paint horse out a little to try to head a cow and the horse just fell over dead right there under him. Richard and J.B. started giving him a hard time about it and Finis got fighting mad. It don't pay to razz a cowboy about his horse, especially when it's lying there dead.

Don recalls learning a lot of lessons in living and doing the right thing from Artie during the time he worked with him. One day they were over on the West Ranch helping with some cattle and Artie happened to ask Richard Pitmon about a ditch he was going to have dug for a water line.

"I thought you were going to get Harry Williams to dig that ditch last week," he said.

"I was going to," Richard replied. "But I can't get him out here to do it. He's probably too drunk to work anyway."

"Now you know Harry is the best guy around when it

comes to digging ditches," Artie said. "He's the best hay hauler around too. He'll get around to it if you give him time."

That response made a big impression on a young man and Don learned from it. Artie never said anything bad about Harry and praised him for what he did well. "Come to think of it," Don said. "I never heard him say anything bad about anyone anytime."

Top row left to right--- Artie and Janet take a break by Pennington Creek, Artie and Janet in front of the house on the East Ranch. Bottom row left to right---Artie and Janet in the buggy, Artie and Janet feed the Brahmas

One Sunday night, Artie and Ag had gone to church in Mill Creek. Don Payne had ridden in with them from the ranch and attended church that morning. After church, he spent the afternoon with his mother and father and then met Artie and Ag at the church that night for a ride back out to the ranch. Artie was driving the 1953 Chevrolet they had just purchased a couple of weeks earlier. Everything went along just fine until they left the county road and started down the pasture road to the ranch house.

For some reason, cows find that the best place to lie down is right in the middle of the road and they were doing a better job than normal of doing that very thing. Time after time, Artie would have to stop, blow the car horn and holler until the cows would get up and move out of the way. This went on all the way through the pasture to the house and it seemed like they were never going to get home. About the time they thought they were through all the cows, they came upon an old bull lying smack in the middle of the road. There was no way to circle around him so Artie started blowing the horn. Surprisingly, the bull got right up and moved to the side of the road. He headed down into the ditch just as they were easing by, but something spooked him and he backed up suddenly hitting the side of the car with his massive hindquarters. The crunching sound was easy to hear inside the car, and sure enough when they got out to look, the side of the car was caved in. That was the final straw for Ag. She started to testify about the sorry qualities of that particular bull and what she'd like to do to him but Artie was unfazed.

"That old bull didn't do that on purpose," he said. "He didn't have any idea what he was doing. Just got scared of something, that's all. Things like this are just going to happen. Don't worry about it."

Don figured the best thing for him to do was just sit there and not say anything, so that's exactly what he did. When they finally got to the ranch house, Ag was still going on about the bull. Don thought he heard her mention something about the bull's ancestry, but he wasn't sure. As he headed for the bunkhouse, he was just hoping the bull incident was forgotten about by breakfast time. He might be able to forgive the bull for smashing in the side of Artie's car, but if that bull caused him to miss one of Ag's breakfasts, that was a different matter altogether.

Don and some of his buddies did get into a little bit of a touchy situation along about that time. They had accidently stumbled onto how Richard Pitmon managed to always have a half-pint bottle of whisky in his boot top. Don was headed up the highway along the west side of the ranch and noticed Fuzzy Carlue doing something along the fence line next to the road. When Fuzzy left, Don went to see what he was doing and found a half-pint bottle of whisky there by the fence post. He left it there and pretty soon, here came Richard riding up and he got down and retrieved the whiskey, shoving it down in the top of his boot. Richard would leave the money tacked to the bottom of the fence post; Fuzzy would leave the whiskey and get the money. Pretty slick deal.

Don mentioned the episode to a couple of his friends in town one day and they decided they would intercept the next whiskey drop. A few days later, they happened to spot Fuzzy making another drop. After he left, they sneaked down and got the bottle of whisky. When Richard came to pick up the bottle, there was, of course, nothing there. He figured Fuzzy had just taken the money without leaving the whisky, so he headed to town to confront him. Don and his buddies hadn't expected that kind of a response from Richard. Richard and Fuzzy argued for a while and then came to some kind of an agreement. Fuzzy let it be known around town that if he found out who had raided his whisky cache, there would be hell to pay. Don and his buddies figured they had better let well enough alone. They never raided another one of Fuzzy's whiskey drops.

Top row left to right--- Artie, Nellie Quinton, Pierce Quinton, Janet, RP Quinton.—House on the West Ranch east of the corrals.
Bottom row left to right---Artie and Janet take a buggy ride, Janet and her dog.

One of the things Don remembers the most about his stay with Artie and Ag is Ag's chocolate cake. It was the best he ever ate and he has never tasted any as good since.

After he quit working on the ranch and joined the Army, Ag would write to him on a regular basis. He always appreciated her letters. He has a special feeling for Artie and Janet as well to this day. The two plus years he spent working with and living with the Quinton family, will always be a special time in his life. It helped to build a bond between them that is still there today.

In the 1950s, if there was any carpenter work or general maintenance type work to be done on the ranch that the cowboys couldn't do, Dutch Payne was called to come do the work. Dutch was Don Payne's dad and was really handy at fixing almost anything. He would fix doors that wouldn't shut, build shelves and feed bins and things of that nature. When Ag would find out that Dutch was coming, she would make up a list of all the things around the house that needed to be fixed. She'd have Dutch working on clothes washers, electrical gadgets, and just about anything else she could think of that wasn't working to her satisfaction.

Doc Swartz began to work with Artie along about that time as well when he started his veterinary business in Sulphur, Oklahoma. Doc always said there was one thing for sure about Artie, when he called for a vet, he had a sick animal and he wouldn't wait until it was too late to do anything for it. He was always well prepared so everything always went well. They lost a few sick cows and calves over the years, but it was never because Artie wasn't looking out for them the best he knew how.

Since the ranches in the part of the country where Doc worked were scattered out all over central and southern Oklahoma, he figured it would save him a lot of time and trouble if he had a helicopter. He took lessons and got a license and pretty soon you could see him leaving out in the thing headed to one of the far flung ranches to doctor a sick cow or horse. He flew the helicopter for about ten years. At one point, he started having spells that would render him unconscious for a short period of time. He didn't figure that was too good a thing to have happen while flying the helicopter, so he sold it. The doctors never found what was causing the spells and they finally quit happening. Doc worked as a veterinary for fifty-four years. He told me he practiced all that time and never did get it right so he just retired. ***(Author's note: Doc tended sick and injured cattle and horses for me in my younger years and I always thought he got it right.)***

A TIME TO TEST YOUR FAITH

In the year of 1955, there were some good doctors at Valley View Hospital in Ada, but they couldn't diagnose the problem. It started as gall bladder problems, but after Ag's gall bladder was removed, the symptoms continued. The surgeon finally said he thought she was just imagining that she still had the same problems. One afternoon, after several days in the hospital, they brought her chicken for supper.

"I can't eat that chicken," she said.

"Sure you can," the nurse replied. "That's why they operated on you so you could eat the things you like again."

Ag tried to eat the chicken, but it was just as it had been before and she got sick and had severe pain shortly afterward. After ten days, and with no further diagnosis forthcoming, they decided she might as well go home. On the way home, around the town of Roff, she had another bout with the pain.

Artie tried to get her to go back to the hospital, but she had been there as long as she intended to stay. Artie took her to Mill Creek where she stayed with her sister for about a week. She just didn't get any better. He decided he would take her to Ardmore, so he called Tom Cardwell and asked him to get a doctor for her.

When they arrived at the hospital, Mr. Cardwell and the doctor were waiting. He was a relatively young doctor and had done his internship at Scott & White Hospital in Temple, Texas. He gave her some pain medicine and told Artie he could take her home that he thought she would be alright.

"She's likely to have another spell before I can get home with her Doc," he said. "I've seen this happen over and over. We've got to do something for her."

"Well, I can send her to a place where they can help her," he said. "Let's send her to Temple." Mr. Cardwell called Leo Roberts and told him to bring a car over to the hospital and take Artie to Temple.

Artie and Leo started for Temple, Texas at midnight that night in a Roadmaster Buick. Ag went in an ambulance and she arrived there about 6:00 o'clock in the morning. They met her in the emergency room. Artie was a little shocked at the condition of the hospital. He knew they had good doctors, but the conditions were not good at all. There were walkways from one area to another where there were sheet iron walls and a sheet iron roof. I expect they were doing a lot of construction.

After they got her checked in and the paperwork all done, Leo handed Artie a wad of bills.

"Leon (Daube) gave me this money to give to you," he said. "He thought you might need it." There was $400 in bills.

"I sure do appreciate it," Artie replied, handing the money back to Leo. "I'm just going to be down here by myself, and I've got enough money to last me a good spell. You take that money back to Mr. Daube and tell him I said I really appreciate it anyway."

"Well, we might as well go get something to eat then," Leo said. By then it was getting on up in the morning. They drove down to a café they found and went in and sat down. Neither of them thought to put any money in the parking meter. When they came out, they had a ticket on the windshield.

"We'll have to find the police station and pay this ticket," Leo said. They finally found the station and told the officer on duty what had happened.

"Where you boys from? He asked.

"We're from Oklahoma," Artie replied. "From around Ardmore."

"Tell you what I'm going to do," the officer said. "If you'll put a dime in the meter outside, I'll let you off. I'm going to give you directions to a parking lot by the hospital that is pretty cheap and you can park there all day if you need to. So they did and were free to go.

When Artie got back to the hospital room, Ag told him she wanted to visit with folks. They walked down the hall, Artie pushing her in a wheelchair until they found a patient who had some visitors. Ag asked if she could visit with them for a while and they were glad to oblige. Later on, the doctor found out about it and told her not to do that anymore. If she needed someone to visit with or anything else to just call. They were there to help her, so if she needed something, to just call the nurse.

They stayed another four days and nights in the hospital and they ran a battery of tests on her. Leo took the train back to Ardmore and left the car for Artie. They were treating her for acid on the stomach and thought she might have to have surgery. Artie didn't think she was strong enough for surgery, but the doctor said if she could walk around the room she was strong enough for surgery. As it turned out, it looked like the medication was going to do the trick.

They were dismissed from the hospital days later and started home at 9:00 o'clock at night. When they got to Hillsboro, the road split and there were two choices. You could go to the west and through Ft. Worth, or to the right and through Dallas. They decided to go through Dallas. When they topped the hill just south of Dallas and looked down on the city, it looked like all the world was lit up. They made it through Dallas alright and by the time they got to Denton, Ag was tired so they got a room and spent the night.

They got an early start, and got back to Ardmore the next day just as the stores were opening up. They stopped to see Mr. Daube and to get the prescription filled that the doctor had given them when they left the hospital the night before. It cost $1.25 to fill the prescription. Artie said you couldn't buy an ice cream cone for that now-a-days.

"How do you think she's doing Artie?" Mr. Daube wanted to know.

"Well, the doctor said he thought she'd be okay now," he replied.

"Sure does make you feel better when you know everybody is trying to help, doesn't it?"

"It sure does" he replied.

That night, they were back on the ranch and were able to sleep in their own bed for the first time in quite a while.

"God never said it would be easy", Artie said. "But He said He'd be there with you. I knew He was with us during that whole ordeal. We couldn't have made it without Him."

Top row left to right---Artie, Janet, Pa McClure (Ag's Dad)—Artie, Nellie Quinton, Pierce Quinton
Bottom row left to right---Janet and Bonnie Pitmon Clark—Artie, Janet, the Lawson boys

There were a lot of good times on the ranch over the years. On many occasions, Artie, Ag, and Janet would all ride pasture and check the cows together. In the summer, it was common for them to stop and take a swim in the creek and then saddle back up and finish riding the rest of the pastures. They did a lot of squirrel hunting back then as well. Mr. Garrison had a really good squirrel dog they would often use. Though you wouldn't think it today, both Artie and Ag were pretty good pranksters as were a lot of the cowboys. A common thing was tying tin cans to a dog's tail and watch him run. Another thing some of the cowboys would do was tie cat's tails together and throw them over a clothesline and watch them fight. One day, some cowboys on the Thompson Ranch tied a couple of cat's tails together and threw them over a cow's back. Those cats clawed all the hide off that cow's sides before they could get them off of her. Then they had to doctor the cow to keep the screwworms from getting in the wounds.

Another trick cowboys pulled on each other was called the "Hot Foot." They would catch a cowboy asleep in the bunk house with his boots on and they would daub a little of the paste type shoe polish on his boot and set it on fire. Pretty soon it would get hot enough to start burning his foot and up from there he would come cussing and trying to get the boot off. When he found out who did it, and he usually would, he would resort to every means in the book to get even.

Jessie Benny Garrison, ("Horseapple" is what most folks called him,) had a dog he called "Bo Jack." One day Bo Jack showed up at Artie and Ag's house and Ag held him while Artie tied a bucket with rocks in it to his tail. Bo Jack took off like the devil himself was after him, that bucket of rocks clanging and banging behind him. Of course they got a good laugh out of that. A few days later, Ag drove the buggy over to the Garrison place and Bo Jack recognized her sitting in the buggy and wouldn't let her out to open the gate. Who says dogs don't hold grudges?

Frank Gaines would run a baling wire from the spark plug

wire on the truck and stick the other end in a watermelon rind. When he started the truck, the voltage would go into the watermelon rind. The chickens would peck the rind and then run backward squawking something terrible. Before long, they would try it again. Frank would really get a kick out of that.

Not long after they moved to the west side of the ranch, they had a bull get down and he stayed down for several days. They tried about everything they knew to try to make the bull get up, all to no avail. Finally, Artie remembered how the chickens acted when they pecked the charged watermelon rind and he thought he might as well try that on the bull. He ran a length of baling wire from the spark plug wire on the truck and tied the other end to the bull's tail. When he started the truck, the bull bellowed right loud and got up. There's more than one way to skin a cat isn't there?

Another time, Artie had a cow down all winter. He faithfully fed and watered that old cow every day even though he figured there was little to no chance he was going to save her. Leon Daube was by the ranch one day in early January when Artie was getting ready to go take care of the cow.

"What you fixin to do Artie?" he asked.

"I'm gonna feed and water that old cow that's been down so long," Artie replied.

"Yea, Yea," Leon said. "I've heard of cows being down all winter and then get up in the spring." He wanted to encourage Artie to keep feeding the old cow in case by some miracle she finally did get up."

Leon brought a horse and buggy over to the ranch for Ag to drive. The horse was a half thoroughbred horse, a grey horse, and they got a lot of use out of that buggy. Artie would take Ag with him in the buggy to fix fence or repair water gaps. He'd throw a roll of barbed wire and some posthole diggers and such on the back of the buggy and they'd spend the day fixing fence. They would sometimes take a picnic lunch with them and sit under the shade trees and eat and take a nap.

There were a couple of boys working on the ranch and living with Richard Pitmon and they wanted to borrow the buggy to take their girlfriends for a ride. They didn't have much experience with a buggy, and when they hitched the horse up they forgot to snap in the strap that held the buggy back off the horse when going downhill. They got over by the old Davis Crossing, and when they started down the hill, the wagon ran up on the horse. The old horse, though gentle, wasn't used to that and got scared. She kicked the spokes out of the front wheels of the buggy and generally tore it up pretty good. They all came back leading the horse.

When they got the buggy all fixed up, Leon Daube donated it to the Southwest Historical Museum in Ardmore. It is all painted up and restored and can still be seen there today.

The first pickup Artie ever had on the ranch was in 1957. He was sure proud of that truck. He talked about how he enjoyed having it to use and how well he took care of it so it would last a long time.

Artie began serving on the school board in 1958 and served fifteen years. At the time he started, Jack Penner was president, Earnest ***(Chili)*** South was vice-president, Jewell Sikes was treasurer, and George Patrick was the other member.

In the early 1960s the school finally decided it was time for a new gymnasium. The school board made plans to visit several area schools that had just recently built new gyms to sort of get an idea of what the current trends were and what they would likely be able to afford. They gathered at the school early one morning and started on a tour of a half dozen schools. As they started out with Superintendent Harden driving, it soon became apparent that they needed a new driver. Mr. Harden was having all kinds of problems staying awake and had almost run into the ditch a number of times. When they made a pit stop at Stratford, Chili South told Artie he needed to drive. They didn't know hardly how to go about getting Mr. Harden to agree to a driver swap, but they knew they were going to have to do something or they were going to have a wreck and kill all of them.

When they got back to the car, Chile just got under the wheel muttering something about giving the driver a break. In two minutes, Mr. Harden was snoring in the seat beside him. They all gave a sigh of relief.

The school board toured gyms all the way from Purcell to McAlester in eastern Oklahoma that day. The plan they finally came up with was taken from what they saw that day.

The first baccalaureate service Artie served on was in 1959. Ray Dodd became superintendent in the 1963-1964 school term. Artie served for years after that and when his eyesight began to fail, he said he thought it was time for them to find a younger man. Ray Dodd said he would lead him onto the stage if he had to. When Ray Dodd became superintendent, Nadine McKinney was cook at the school. She would always call him "that young kid." Artie told her when she learned "that young kid" was the boss, she'd be fine.

Artie wrote his name in the cement of the barn at West ranch when barn was built in 1948.

THE MAKING OF A MAN

It was a springtime morning on Rock Prairie and the dogwoods along Mill Creek were in full bloom. There was a flurry of activity everywhere. The birds were busy building nests for the hatchlings that were soon to arrive. Two red squirrels were chasing each other through the trees along the creek and a blue jay was scolding them for making such a fuss. It was a time for new birth and of awakening old spirits. The long hard winter was finally over, the creek ran full with the spring rains, and the landscape of brown winter grasses was splotched with patches of new green growth. A flock of wild turkeys made their easy way down a brushy draw toward the creek stopping here and there to feast on the insects that were in abundance in the tall grasses. A lone coyote stood atop the hill just to the north of the draw and watched the turkeys. He had a successful night of hunting and was on his way to the den when he spotted the turkeys. Was it worth the time and effort to try to sneak down and nab one, or should he go on to the den and a well-deserved nap? The sound of something coming through the thick brush west of the creek made up his mind for him. When he saw the young man step out of the brush and stand looking around, he turned and went down the other side of the hill so as not to be seen.

Top row left to right---Artie mounts up—Cowboys bring in the cattle Bottom row left to right---Loading them up to ship—Heading out to the roundup

Young Sam Daube stood and looked over the open area. The area where he stood was originally named the Southwest Mule Pasture, but due to the rough country, Artie had re-named it Tomcat Ridge and the name stuck. Sam could see a fairly good distance in every direction, but there was not a horse in sight. It was time to give up looking. He was going to have to do the one thing no self-respecting cowboy ever wanted to do, walk back to the gathering pens afoot. He was sure to get a lot of good natured ribbing from the rest of the cowboys for losing his horse and he wasn't looking forward to it one little bit. He certainly hadn't meant for it to happen, especially with all the older cowboys around so they were sure to find out.

He had just been riding along looking for cows to drive in to the pens, not paying much attention to where he was going. All of a sudden, something spooked his horse, and before he could get him gathered up, into the brush he went at a full run. He saw the low hanging limb just before it hit him across the chest, but he didn't have time to duck. The next thing he knew, he was picking himself up off the ground. He was skinned up a little, but upon further self-examination, didn't seem to have any broken bones or other serious injuries. Except to his pride, that is. His horse had vanished into the thick brush, and try as he might, he hadn't been able to locate him. There was nothing left to do; so he started toward the gathering pens. It wasn't hard to tell which direction to go, all he had to do was follow the whooping and hollering from the cowboys as they drove the cattle into the pens. As he neared the pens, a cowboy came out of the brush to his right driving a few head of cattle. He recognized Artie Quinton about the same time Artie spotted him standing in the edge of the brush.

"What happened to your horse Sam?" He asked.

"Lost him", Sam replied with a sheepish look on his face. Then he went on to tell how his horse had spooked and ran under the limb.

"Don't worry about it son," Artie replied. "Get on behind

me and we'll find that old horse. Don't you keep that horse in the lot most of the time?"

"Yes sir," Sam replied.

"That horse will be grazing on the first patch of green grass he comes to," Artie said.

Sam climbed on behind and they rode back to the place where he remembered the accident happening. Artie started riding in a big circle and pretty soon they spotted Sam's horse grazing on the new green grass in a little clearing. Sam gathered him up and got back into the saddle.

Now Artie had every opportunity to hurrah him a little and most cowboys would have done that and worse. All Artie said, however, was "Let's go get them cows." That's all that was said of the incident as they went on about the roundup. It is an incident that has stuck in Sam Daube's mind through the years. He remembers how he appreciated what Artie did for him that day and the character he showed in doing it. It was a good learning experience for a green cowboy and Sam never forgot it. He wasn't the first cowboy whose life had been influenced by Artie Quinton. One more thing; he wasn't the last either.

Laurie Williams stayed with Artie and Ag one summer and helped around the ranch just like one of the regular hands. She would get up early in the morning and wash and dry her hair before the workday started and the workday started early. When they would get back to the house in the afternoon, she would jog over to the highway and back for exercise.

They were clearing some land for a green field at the time. Artie would go to Sulphur and pick up a load of old railroad ties and they would set them on fire to burn the brush. They had a forty gallon propane tank mounted on the back of a tractor and would use it to get the railroad ties burning. Laurie would drag as much brush as anybody. She would help brand cattle and Artie let her cut the calves ears to mark them. She stuck a few of the little ear tips in her pocket. She was going home to spend the night and come back the next day. At the supper table that night, she happened to remember having the ear tips in her pocket and she took them out to show her parents what she had been doing that day. That just about ruined the supper that night.

Laurie was a freshman at Purdue University that year. Carol Daube Sutton was her grandmother and her mother's name was Ida. Laurie owns the Ranch where Artie retired these days and leases it out to Clyde Runyan. She is also a lawyer and is a champion of the initiative to protect the water in the Arbuckle Simpson Aquifer.

There were a lot of small Bois de' arc trees just east of the ranch house. (We always called them Horse apple trees when I was growing up.) By that time they had a big John Deere tractor on the place and one day Artie was throwing a chain on the back of the tractor when Leon Daube came driving up.

"What you fixin' to do Artie?" He asked.

"I was thinking I might take the tractor and pull up a few of those Bois de' arc trees," Artie replied.

"You can't pull up a tree without messing up the grass a little can you?" Leon asked.

"Well, I don't think it will mess up as much grass as leaving the tree there will," Artie ventured.

"Tell you what we'll do," Leon said. "I'll send somebody over here with some of them pellets. They're supposed to kill a Bois de' arc tree. Be a lot easier than trying to pull them up with a tractor.

When Artie retired, the trees were a lot bigger and had never had any of the pellets put around them.

Artie talks a lot about cattle ranching in his day and how it has evolved over the years. He is quick to tell you that he doesn't know anything about the ranching techniques in use on a lot of ranches today. He will, however, describe what he thinks you have to do to make it in the cattle business. The first thing he talks about is physical responsibility and the need to be conservative. For many years on the ranch, the only way to do anything with a cow or calf, or bull for that matter, was to rope it and get it down on the ground. They worked calves that way, branded that way, and everything else that needed to be done to a cow was done that way. When they finally got a branding table, Leon Daube talked about how they had done it the hard way all those years. "About time to make it a little easier," he said.

Mostly, ranching in the early to middle years of the 20th century was just plain old hard work. Digging post holes by hand across the rocky hillsides to put up a fence was really a job. Jewell Sikes remarked one time that he worked three whole days with a bar and posthole diggers trying to get a posthole for a corner post four feet deep. I can't think of much harder work than that.

"Seems like the winters were harder back in the 1920s and 1930s,"Artie said. "I remember having to feed on foot because a horse couldn't stand up if you got him out on the icy ground." They finally learned to grind an angle on the calks of the horse shoes that would help the horses get better footing on the ice. In the feed pen days, when the steers were gone to market, the bare dirt in the pens would freeze over and a horse or cow couldn't stand up at all.

Artie says one of the most important things about a ranch is the water supply. If you don't have good water, you aren't likely to make it in the ranching business. There would be someone come around every year or so on the ranch and check the depth of the water table. Over the years, the water level was seen to be lowering and probably still is today. He is concerned that folks are going to sell water out of the aquifer and destroy the water supply needed for this area. "You've got to take care of your water," he said. "We're already using it faster than the good Lord is making it."

The best well on the entire ranch was at the feed pens. In the 1930s and early 1940s, the well at the feed pens would supply water for as many as 900 head of steers on dry feed and 200 hogs. It would sometimes run as high as twelve to fourteen hours a day. It was rigged with an old oil field type pump with a 3 inch output line coming out of it. There were two 250 gallon storage tanks built on stands above and to the side of the well for emergency water in case it was ever needed. You would just close the valve going to the watering troughs and that would force the water up into the tanks.

There were a lot of dry years on the ranch, but the driest Artie could remember was 1956. Pilot springs went dry and the whole length of Pennington Creek was dry. You could ride a horse up the creek bed from the bridge at Gray's Ranch all the way to the headwaters on Turner Ranch and never get his feet wet. "Years like that will teach you to conserve the water," he said.

"A lot of folks go about handling cattle a lot differently today," he said. "I went up to the Jacob Ranch to watch them brand a few years back and they would head and heel a calf and get him down and brand him. That way is a lot of fun, but it is losing you money at the same time. If you are losing a couple of pounds each off of several hundred head of cattle, you're talking about a lot of money thrown away. Cattle are a lot like people, the better you treat them, the better you're going to get along with them."

In the early 1970s, Daube Ranch decided the best way to upgrade their fine herd of Hereford cattle was through artificial insemination. This would be a new endeavor for them and they needed someone with expertise in the field to do the inseminations. Doc Easley was serving as veterinary for Winrock Farms at the time, and was contracted to do the job. Doc had started with Turner Ranch and when the ranch changed owners, he stayed on. He was also an expert in artificial insemination.

Doc went down to visit with Artie to set up the routine for the inseminations. It was an everyday affair, and needed to be done at a certain time. A lot of vets thought 5:00 o'clock in the afternoon was the optimum time for insemination, but Doc was partial to 2:00 o'clock, so that was the time chosen.

Doc and Artie proved to be a good team. Doc would show up promptly at the prescribed time every day, and Artie would have the cows that were to be inseminated up in the corral and ready to go. For the most part, the artificial insemination program was a success and produced many show calves and club calves as well as breeding stock to augment the herd. The program went on for about three years then the decision was made to discontinue it. The successful birth rate was just not quite as good as they would have liked, and it took a lot of time that needed to be spent doing other duties on the ranch.

Top row left to right---Artie and an unidentified cowboy sorting them out—Artie helping them down the chute
Bottom row left to right---Loading them up (something is funny to Artie)—Artie heading them back out to pasture

Often when the work was done, there would be time for a

glass of Ag's iced tea and a seat in the shade. On one occasion, Artie happened to mention a calf that was down on his feed and didn't seem to be getting any better.

"I've got this calf that just started going down and losing weight," he said. "Took him down to Tishomingo to the vet and he kept him, three, maybe four days and said he'd be alright. He just don't seem to be getting any better though. I'm afraid he's not going to make it. You want to have a look at him Doc?"

They walked out to where the cow was grazing in a little trap by the corral. The calf was with her, but it was easy to tell the thing wasn't up to snuff.

"Tell you what," Doc said. "You have that cow and calf both up when I get here tomorrow, and when we get through with the inseminations; I'll take a look at her.

When Doc arrived at the ranch the next day, he could see the cow and the sick calf in the lot next to the cows to be inseminated. When the work was all done, he asked Artie to run the cow and calf both into the chute.

"What you think Doc?" Artie asked after Doc had looked the calf over good.

Doc continued to run his hands over the calf's legs and chest. He listened with the stethoscope and then took the calf's temperature.

"I'm a good mind to give this calf a blood transfusion," he said.

"A transfusion!" Artie exclaimed. "Why, I never heard of giving a calf a transfusion. Where you gonna get the blood from?"

"We're gonna get it from the momma cow," Doc said. "Let's get her head in the head gate."

Doc commenced to stick that cow in the neck with a big needle and soon enough they had a quart bottle full of blood. Then he fed that bottle of blood through the tube into a vein in the calf's neck.

"You watch that calf now," he told Artie. I want a report every day on how that calf is doing. Shouldn't take but a few days to see if this is going to help or not.

Sure enough, the next day, Artie was sure the calf was a little better. Then the second day, he reported she was better still. On the third day, Artie pronounced the calf completely healed and as good as new. It was the first time Artie had seen blood transfusion in cattle. Doc admitted later that he didn't know if it would work, but since everything else had been tried, it was the only thing he could think of.

Doc Easley and Artie Quinton have been friends all these many years since. They both spent many years working on a ranch and working with livestock. They have a lot of respect for one another to this day, and they are both quick to give praise to the other. They are among the last of a dying breed of cowboy that has endured since the days of the famous cattle drives and working for the brand. They are both closing in on the century mark; Doc is 95 years old this year and Artie will turn 98 years old this October 2010. They will both tell you they never heard the other say an unkind word toward anyone. They are both fine Christian gentlemen and stand as examples of what is good and kind in this world. I am truly fortunate to know them and call them friend.

A ROUGH TUMBLE

The Spring Creek Ranch at Reagan was one of the wooliest pieces of property Daubes owned. It might not match parts of the Rock Prairie Ranch for pure dee rough country, but it rivaled any other spread around that part of the country for how tough it was to get stock out of. It wasn't a big ranch, as ranches go, and it didn't carry as many cows as the other ranches mostly due to the amount of timber and rocky stretches it enclosed.

Having said that, it was one of the prettiest places around. It was aptly named for the crystal clear waters of the creek that got its name from the many springs that flowed into it and kept it running and the waters clear.

In the time period that Jim Crenshaw ran the Spring Creek Ranch for Daube's, the ranch only supported around 150 head of mother cows. Jim was there for about two and a half years starting in 1975. It was a chore to gather those 150 cows whenever it came time for working the calves, shipping, or any of the other sundry things that required the cows to be brought to the corrals. It was a common thing for cowboys to come in with cuts, scrapes, abrasions, and such just from hazing the cows out of the brush and timber. Occasionally, there would be something of a more serious nature happen and one of those instances scared all the crew, including Jim's wife Vicky, pretty badly.

Fall of the year on Spring Creek meant that deer hunting season was just around the corner. The trees were decked out in their fall splendor of reds, browns, and golds. There was a chill to the early morning air as the four cowboys headed out from the ranch house to gather the cows. There were calves to be shipped, keeper heifers to be branded, cows to be culled, and the last of that year's calf crop to be worked and vaccinated. Deer hunting would just have to wait.

They would split up in pairs to better work the cattle out of the brush and keep them headed to the corrals. Bob Crenshaw and Jim Hook headed to the east side of the ranch and Artie and Jim Crenshaw would start at the north end and push everything on that side down the creek and cross just below the corrals. At least that was the plan. Ain't it funny how plans don't always go just the way we think they will?

Jim Crenshaw was riding a horse that Sam Daube had brought over for him to ride and he hadn't been on him too many times. Everything started out well and by the time Artie and Jim broke out of the timber above the crossing with a good bunch of cows and calves, they could see Bob and Jim Hook just coming around the corner of the timber east of the creek.

They had about fifty head of cows in front of them and were lined out to meet up with them at the crossing.

The trail leading down to the crossing on Spring Creek was fairly steep on the west side and the cows bunched up pretty good as they made the crossing. Artie followed them through and Jim Crenshaw was right behind. There were several fair sized rocks sticking out of the water at the crossing, and those rocks were all wet from the water splashing everywhere as the cattle crossed the creek. When the iron clad hooves of Jim's horse hit the first rock, it was like stepping on ice and down he went into the creek with Jim still aboard. He rolled over Jim and as he did, one of his hooves hit Jim in the back of the head. The iron horseshoe cut a gash long and deep and blood started flowing out of that gash at an alarming rate.

Artie and the other two cowboys all plunged into the creek and got Jim up and out of the way of the struggling horse. The horse managed to right himself and finally got to his feet, apparently unharmed. Artie got Jim up on his horse and got on behind him to support him on the ride to the house. The cattle started on to the house and they followed slowly behind. Jim kept asking if his horse was alright and Artie kept telling him to not worry about the horse. "We're not worried about that horse right now," he said. "Let's just get you to the house so we can see how badly you're hurt."

Vicky looked out the kitchen window where she had been fixing dinner and saw them coming. When she saw Jim, his shirt and face all bloody, riding with Artie she knew something bad had happened. She ran out to meet them and helped Artie bring Jim into the house. They stuck his head under the faucet and washed away the blood enough to see the cut on his head.

Vicky pressed a cloth to the wound to help stop the bleeding and they put him in the car and headed to Sulphur and the hospital emergency room.

With a large shaved spot in the back of his head, and a neat row of stitches to close the gap, Jim was soon about as good as new. At least good enough to help finish the roundup later that afternoon. He still has a visible scar today from that little episode in Spring Creek. Vicky said it was the only time she ever saw Artie flustered. He was always so calm in all situations, but the injury really shook him up. I think it is his natural concern for other people that made him upset. It would not be the last Spring Creek injury, but it was the worst one while Jim worked there. He was mighty lucky; the blow could have done a lot more damage than it did. Just another day in the life of a cowboy.

Jim rode that horse a lot after that. In fact, he rode him so much of the time that when they finished shipping the next year, Artie told him he wanted to take the horse to his place for a little while to let him rest up.

"You've been riding that horse so much you've got him wore plumb down," he told Jim. He took him home with him and kept him for a couple of weeks and brought him back. Jim saddled up and mounted just like he always did. That horse broke in two and bucked him off. He got up off the ground and gave Artie a funny look. "I guess he wasn't as worn down as I thought he was," Artie said with a grin.

Artie, Jim Crenshaw, and Jim Hook were riding pasture on Spring Creek one day and ran across a sick cow. They believed she had anaplasmosis and decided to drive her to the corral so she could be doctored and seen after on a daily basis. They started her slowly toward the corral and were just following along after her. They were almost to the corrals when she lost her nerve and went to fighting the horses. Jim Crenshaw was riding a big old horse that day. The old cow turned and ran at Jim's horse and caused him to rear up. He came down on top of the cow with most of his weight.

"Well, there's a dead cow," Artie said. Sure enough, when Jim went out to check on her later that night, she was dead.

Occasionally, despite all you can do, calves are going to catch something or get sick. They were gathering cattle on the West Ranch one day and as they neared to corrals, they noticed a couple of calves lagging behind. It was plain to see they both had pneumonia. The last thing you want to do with a calf that has pneumonia is to get it hot. They eased one of the calves into the corral being careful not to hurry it any more than they had to. Meanwhile, Sam Daube rode up and saw the other calf outside the corral, so he roped it and dragged it into the corral.

"Sam Daube, you just killed that calf," Artie hollered. "You just more than likely killed that calf by doing that."

Jim Crenshaw heard what he said and was a little shocked that Artie would say what he did to the man that owned the calves and paid their salary to boot. Sam coiled up his rope, tied his horse to the fence and walked over and started talking to Artie just like nothing happened. They had a mutual respect for each other and both knew Artie had the best interest of the cattle at heart. It's hard to be unhappy with a man that is taking care of your stock like Artie did.

Every person that worked with Sam Daube on the ranch had nothing but good things to say about him. He would jump in and help just like all the cowboys and if you didn't know Sam, you wouldn't know which one of the cowboys he was. Several former Daube hands declare Sam Daube to be as good a hand as they ever worked around. That's fine praise from a bunch of real cowboys.

Artie worked with Jim Hook for 16 years. Sadly, Jim passed away in July 2010 and was not in good enough health the last few weeks of his life to talk about his experiences with Artie over the many years they worked together. Artie said there were three things that stuck in his mind about Jim. You weren't going to get him excited, you weren't going to get him in a hurry, and he was going to be there every day.

Jim was working at the Rock Prairie Ranch for a while and was starting a bunch of heifers. Sam Daube happened by one day and they walked out to look at the heifers. They were pretty skittish that day, more than likely due to seeing somebody with Jim that they weren't used to.

"Looks to me like if you'd spend a little more time around them heifers, they would be a little more calm," Sam said.

"If seven days a week is not good enough for you Sam, then you can just get somebody else," Jim replied. Sam liked to have never got through apologizing to Jim about that remark.

Sam Daube thought a lot of Jim and after Jim retired his knowledge and cow savvy were really missed on the ranch. Sam finally talked him into coming back to work for a while to help out some of the young guys and get them started right.

Jim told Don Payne one time that Artie must have not kept him very busy when he worked on the East Ranch, because he had found his name carved all over the old bunkhouse and saddle shop. He got a kick out of teasing Don about it.

Since Artie knew about everybody in the country, it was pretty much of a sure bet that Tom Cardwell, Leo Roberts, and even Sam Daube would ask him about what kind of a hand a prospective employee was likely to be. Sam asked Artie one time about a young man that had grown up in the Mill Creek area. He was thinking about hiring the young man but wanted Artie's opinion before he did.

"What do you know about this guy Artie?" Sam asked.

"Well, I'll tell you," Artie replied. "You won't get him in a hurry, but he'll be on the job every day. He's a pretty fair mechanic too."

About three months after that conversation, they were gathering cattle on the West Ranch and Sam mentioned the talk they had earlier. "You remember telling me about the young man I hired here awhile back don't you Artie?"

"Yea, I remember talking about him," Artie replied.

"There's one thing you didn't tell me about him," Sam said. "He's lazy."

"I figured you'd find that out on your own," Artie replied with a grin.

Mike Pitmon worked with Artie on the ranch for a period of time back in the 1970's. He found Artie to have a sense of humor and also a little bit of the prankster about him. Kenneth

Converse had a few old mules on his place and they were forever getting out and would end up on Daube's land part of the time. They were a nuisance to say the least and would always be right in the way when they were trying to do something with the cattle. One day one of the mules was there right in the way like normal and they had put up with him all they intended to. The old mule was kicking at them and trying to bite and about everything else a mule might do, but they final captured him. Just for fun, they tied an empty metal five gallon bucket to his tail with a piece of baling wire and turned him loose. That old mule went to bucking and snorting and raising all kinds of a fuss. Artie was bent over and slapping his knees he was laughing so hard. As a matter of fact, he was laughing so hard that he didn't see the mule coming for him and he was barely able to get out of the way in time. Mike almost got ran over himself trying to get out of Artie's way. The mule finally jumped the cattle guard and headed down the road toward home. They didn't see him on Daube land again. I can't say as I blame him; I wouldn't hang around that kind of treatment very long myself.

The devil worked on Artie just like he does everybody. He has always volunteered the same advice about what to do when you've done something wrong or just something you're not too proud of. "I find that when I get wrong, I stay wrong until I get right." What he really means by that statement is that you have to get down on your knees and ask God for forgiveness for whatever it was that you did that you shouldn't have done.

One day Mike and Artie were working some cattle and there was a commotion that started out of Mike's range of sight so he wasn't quite sure what had happened. It appeared that something had happened involving Artie's horse. Pretty soon, Artie turned up missing. He hadn't said a word to Mike about anything, but he just wasn't there. The corral full of cattle were all milling around and Mike began to worry that Artie had fallen in under the cattle. As he made his way through the cattle he began to hear sounds coming from behind the big round water trough. As he got closer, he could tell it was Artie and he was kneeling behind the trough and was praying. He was getting back right for something. That made a big impression on Mike and he has never forgotten it.

Mike was riding pasture one day and ran across a little tiny premature born calf. That thing wasn't any bigger than a full grown Jack rabbit. He gathered it up and put it on the saddle in front of him and rode back to the barn. When he got back to the barn, he fixed a bottle of calf manna and was trying to get the calf to drink some of it when Artie came walking up.

"Let me do that Mike," Artie said.

"Naw, I've got it," Mike replied. It was only a few seconds until Artie tried again.

"Let me do it Mike," he said.

"I'm okay," Mike answered and kept on trying to get the calf to swallow some of the milk. Finally, Artie had enough.

"Let me show you how to do that," he said. There was nothing else to do so Mike let him take over. Artie pulled the calf's tongue out and told Mike to pour some of the milk in the calf's mouth. Mike poured in a little milk, but he could see the calf wasn't swallowing so he quit pouring.

"Pour in a little more," Artie said. Mike poured in a little more and stopped again.

"Keep pouring it in," Artie said. "I'll tell you when to stop."

Mike poured in the milk until he could see the calf's eyes begin to roll back in his head. "We're gonna drown him I believe," he said. Artie took the calf by the hind legs and shook him a little to see if he could get any reaction from him. When he stopped shaking him, the calf just lay there.

"Mentally retarded anyway," Artie said. With that, he headed back to the house.

Not all cowboys that hired on for Daube's would make the grade. The cowboy life with all its glamour is still a lot of hard work. The hours are long most of the time and cows have to be tended and fed seven days a week. Odell Webb had a brother that hired on and was one that found out pretty quick that he needed to find another line of work. The company had given him a good saddle to ride and when he left they found that he had carved his name into the seat of the saddle. As it turned out, if that carving was ever gonna get worn off, it would be another cowboy's behind that did the wearing, not his.

A big part of any working cattle ranch is the horse herd. A ranch horse is one of the tools a ranch hand uses in his work most every day in some way or another. They form a partnership, working together to get the job done. Most every cowboy has a favorite horse, one he feels more comfortable with than any other.

The Daube Ranch had a lot of good horses over the many

years Artie worked on the ranch. In the early days of Artie's employment with the ranch, horses were a commodity just like the cattle were. If someone came along and wanted to buy a horse, and if the price could be agreed on, then the horse was sold. It didn't matter which cowboy the horse might be assigned to, the sale was made. That cowboy would be assigned another horse to ride.

There was one occasion though, when that system didn't work out. Richard Pitmon was riding a blue roan horse that he was really proud of. He had spent a lot of time training that horse and could do anything a cowboy needed to do horseback on that horse. Pug Croskil was at the ranch one day and watched Richard working some cattle on the horse and he told Tom Cardwell he wanted to buy the horse. They dickered around a little and finally settled on a price. The horse was delivered to his new owner without Richard's knowledge, and when he found out about it, he threw a fit. He threw a real tantrum, threatened to whip somebody, then finally decided he would just quit if Tom didn't go get the horse back. To make a long story short, Tom went back to Pug with his hat in his hand, and asked if he could buy the horse back. After hearing the reason, Pug agreed to sell the horse back to him. The price Tom bought the horse back for was never divulged. Richard didn't care though. He had his horse back and that was what he wanted.

In the early years, all the horses on the ranch were broke to ride by the ranch hands themselves and they did all the shooing as well. "Victor Lee" was a stud horse and sired many good horses that ended up working on the ranch. One of the best mares that he sired was named "Bonnie Lee" out of a mare named "Bonnie."

Mr. Daube brought a little dun horse and a big bay horse over for them to use on the ranch and said they were green broke. The bay horse was hump backed and Artie said right off that he wouldn't be any good because of that hump back. Sure enough, his back would get sore every time you rode him. Jim Hook took the little horse they later named "Pig Pen." Artie figured he was too small to be a good cow horse. That little dun horse would buck like nobody's business. He would buck in a circle and squeal like a pig, thus the name "Pig Pen." Jim finally got him to handling pretty well and one day they were bringing in some cows and Pig Pen got all bent out of shape and went to bucking. They happened to be in a rocky area, and that horse came down wrong on a rock and split his front hoof all the way to the quick. Artie took him to Sulphur to Doc Swartz, and he fixed him up as best he could. It took him several months to completely get over it and when Jim finally went to riding him again, he started the bucking right where he left off. Jim had finally had enough of old Pig Pen.

"Artie, I don't believe I want to ride that horse anymore," he said.

"I don't blame you son," Artie replied. "You've got a wife and kids to think about." Looks like old Pig Pen won that one, don't it?

Duter Conner broke one horse that had a knot on his jaw so they just named him "Knot." Sounds like a lot of imagination went into that name don't it? A good horse with a flaxen mane and tail was just *called "Flax."* There was one horse they called "Spider," and Don Payne rode him a lot.

There was a team of work horses on the ranch as well. They were named "Ed" and "Gotch." At one time, Gotch had screwworms in one ear and they almost ate it off leaving him "gotch eared". They were big horses. Ed weighed in around 1540 pounds and Gotch at 1480 pounds.

Ag would mostly ride a horse named "Doggie" and she would sometimes have three or more kids on with her. "Cactus Pete" was probably the best roping horse on the ranch. There was a horse named "Hawk" that was a bucker. Artie was on him one day and Mr. Cardwell, Harmon Clark, and Richard Pitmon were watching the show. They said he was bucking so hard it was hard for them to watch. ***(The full story of that ride is included in an earlier chapter).*** That may give you a hint of how good a rider Artie was in his prime. At the time he retired, Artie was riding a pair of red roans. He called them "Strawberry" and "Cornstalk". They gave him his saddle when he retired and his grandson Billye Bob still uses it today. Over the years, Artie and Ag had seventeen different boys stay with them and work on the ranch.

They always had a milk cow on the ranch and Ag sold a lot of milk. Some folks were really particular about their milk. Effie Spears wouldn't take anything but morning milk, thinking it was better than evening milk. When the Quintons took a trip to California one year, Janet's husband Bobby did the milking for them while they were gone. He would mix the morning milk and the evening milk together and she never knew the difference. Travis Vaughan bought a lot of milk for his family as well. When Artie retired, Janet took the milk cow to the Sheep Ranch where she and Bobby lived and milked her for another two years.

Artie talks a lot about the people he worked for over the years at Daubes. He worked for three generations of Daubes. He started to work for the Old Man Sam Daube in 1937. Sam died in 1946 and his son Leon took over the ranch. Leon died in 1956. He was a super person and Artie considered him a very personal friend. After Leon Daube passed away, Tom Cardwell took over as General Manager of all the ranches. He had been working for Daube Ranches since the 1920's. Tom died in 1965 of a heart attack as he was driving down the road. Leo Roberts took over after that. One day when Leo's grandson Blake was about five years old, Leo brought him with him on a visit to Artie's. Artie thought Blake favored his grandpa a lot and he told him so.

"Blake, you're going to look just like your grandpa when you get grown," he said.

"Golly, like that!" He replied. You could tell he wasn't too excited about that prospect.

Leo actually started working on the ranch in 1952 and took over as General Manager in 1965. He had married a woman from Ardmore named Jimmie Hill. Her father was one of the owners of Hill & Shipe's Shoe Store. Leo and Jimmie went to Montana and he worked on a big ranch up there for a while. He soon got tired of the brutal winters and they moved back to Ardmore. Jimmie had her mind made up that he was going to be a shoe salesman. Leo just wasn't cut out to be a shoe salesman, so when the opportunity came along to go to work for the Daube Ranches, he jumped at the chance. He worked for Daubes over fifty years and passed away in 2008. At the time he retired, Artie was working for the younger Sam Daube, son of Leon and Olive Daube.

"These were all super people and I never had a cross word from any of them," Artie said.

The only time he ever really had a disagreement with any of his bosses was one time when he and Leroy Pitmon were riding pasture and spotted a big old steer with screw worms in a wound at the base of one horn. Tom Cardwell happened along about the time Artie was shaking out a loop to throw on the steer. He meant to rope him and doctor him right then and there. Tom Cardwell told him he didn't think he ought to rope him because he was just too big to handle.

"Just drive him to the lot," he said. "We'll doctor him and watch him a few days." Then he went on about his business.

Now a real cowboy just doesn't like to miss a good opportunity to tie onto something, and that steer really did need to be doctored. Artie figured with the time it was going to take to drive him all the way to the corral, doctor him and get back down here, he wasn't going to have time to look over the rest of the cows. So what did he do? Why he threw a loop on that old steer just like he wanted to do in the first place. Problem was, it didn't go just like he had it figured. He dropped the loop on that steer just as he hit the brand new barbed wire fence. Luckily, he hit the fence right where they had put in a wire gate and he just rode the gate down to the ground as he went over it. The steer got his legs tangled up in the wire and down he went.

Artie managed to tie him down before he could get untangled and gave the infected horn a good doctoring. That steer had gotten a mess of wire cuts when he ran through that wire gate, and they needed doctoring pretty badly as well. That was just about the time old Doc Begaars came out with a new cut salve, and Artie usually carried some of it in his saddlebag in case he needed to doctor something out in the pasture. He smeared the salve on all of the cuts before he turned that old steer loose. He finally managed to get the steer out of the mess of wire and turned him loose. He really figured he would come up with the rest of the stock for feed the next day and he'd put him in the lot if he needed to be doctored more.

The next day, the steer didn't come up for feed with the rest of the cows. When he didn't come up the second day and the feeding was all taken care of, Artie figured they better go look for him. He and Leroy saddled a couple of horses and went looking for the steer. They found him close to where they had left him a couple of days earlier. The steer was stove up considerable from the fall and the various wire cuts he received when he went through the gate. The salve had blistered him pretty good as well, and had taken some of the hide off around the cuts. Artie managed to get him up and they started him slowly back to the ranch house and the corral. They were taking him right up the side of the gravel road that ran to the ranch house. Before they had gone far, they heard a car coming up the road behind them and when he turned to look, Artie could see it was Tom Cardwell. Tom pulled up along the side of the road about even with him and stopped the car and got out.

"What happened to him Artie?" He asked.

Wasn't nothing else to do but tell it like it was, so that's what

Artie did. When he finished telling what had happened, Mr. Cardwell dropped his right shoulder and tapped the toe of his boot like he was prone to do just before he spoke.

"I don't believe I'd do that anymore," he said. "You usually get in trouble." With that, he got in the car and drove off. He had every right to really give him a chewing out but he knew how best to handle the situation. He knew men as well as he knew cattle. Artie will tell you to this day, he appreciated Mr. Cardwell handling it like he did and he never forgot it.

Artie always thought it was important to track the quality of calves a cow would have year after year. He would watch the calves and the cows they went with and if a cow had a good quality calf every year, she was sure enough a keeper. On the other hand, if she had a little knot headed calf every year or every so often, it was probably to their benefit to get rid of that particular cow.

They were all down at the Rock Prairie Ranch shipping cattle one fall and Tom Cardwell asked Odell Webb, the foreman at Rock Prairie, what cow a little calf went with.

"What cow does that little runt calf go to Odell?" He asked.

"Why, I don't know," Odell answered.

"Wait 'til we get up to Artie's," Tom answered. "He'll know.

Odell didn't care too much for that comment, but Tom really didn't mean anything by it, he was just stating a fact.

There are a few things that are really important to a cowboy as he goes about his work. One of those things is his saddle. Artie was riding a shop made saddle that was made at the Randolph Saddle Shop. Leon Daube gave him the saddle and he rode it for a long time. As he started getting older, he needed a saddle with a little more support in the front and the back. Sam Daube was at the ranch one day and he told Sam he could sure use a different saddle if he ran across one that had a little more support to it. Frank Preston was with Sam and when they started home, Frank looked at Sam. "Do you know what your daddy would have done if Artie had asked him what he asked you?" He said.

"No, I don't reckon I do," Sam replied.

"He'd of gone and bought him a new saddle," Frank said.

It wasn't long after that they were branding up at Artie's place.

"Have you got time to go with me to Ardmore when we get through branding today Artie? Sam asked. "I want to show you something."

They went to Ardmore and Sam took Artie to the Randolph Saddle Shop. He showed him a saddle and told him it was the one he picked out for him, but if he didn't like it, to pick any saddle in the place. Artie liked the saddle but he told Sam he didn't need the fancy sheep-lined flank girth. "You can save a few dollars there," he said. Artie was still riding that saddle when he retired.

PART SEVEN: A HEALING FROM GOD 1976-1984

December 1976 brought the most traumatic period of Artie and Ag's married life. The day started out much like any other day. They were doing a lot of artificial insemination at the time and Artie was in the habit of rising early and would be out in the little twenty acre trap before daylight getting the cows in that would be bred that day. He was also doing a lot of reading in the Bible every morning. He would get up early enough to read three full chapters before he started his day's work.

He wasn't feeling exactly right that morning as he headed down to the barn to milk. The first thing that gave him any indication that all was not well was when he passed out and then came to on the ground in the stall with the milk cow. He knew he needed to get to one side of the stall or the other so he could cling to the wall as he tried to stand up. He couldn't remember if he had finished milking or not. He always hung the full milk pail on a certain nail while he let the cow out of the stable and when he looked over to the nail, the milk pail was hanging there. He was finally able to stand upright, but his head was hurting something awful. He somehow managed to let the cow out into the trap, take the milk pail down from the nail, and head for the house. He managed to open the lot gate and the yard gate on the way to the house. He went in through the garage like normal and deposited the milk pail where he always put it for Ag to handle later.

When he entered the kitchen, Ag could tell something was wrong with him. He told her his head was hurting really bad so she told him to sit down and she would call one of the boys to go to the corral. There was a man from Ardmore at the ranch helping out and his name was Harold Parker. He came up to the house and they loaded Artie up and headed for the hospital at Ardmore. Ag had called Janet and they met her before they got to the highway. Artie sat up all the way to the hospital, but by the time they got him to the Adventist Hospital, he was in a comma. Carol Daube Sutton met them at the hospital. Dr. Turrentine was on vacation so they got a doctor named Dr. Patkowsky to see Artie.

"What are you going to do with him Doc?" Carol asked.

"I'd like to take him over to Memorial Hospital and do a brain scan and an arteriogram but he's not able," he replied.

"Well, ***do something*** then," Carol said.

"Lady, I'm not sure there is anything I can do," he said.

"Then let's get him to Oklahoma City or Temple, Texas," she said.

They called Oklahoma City and talked with the doctors at

St. Anthony Hospital and at 12:00 o'clock midnight they loaded him into an ambulance and headed for Oklahoma City. Artie remained in a coma all the way to the hospital. When they arrived, he went in for a brain scan and an arteriogram. The two radiologists that did the brain scan came out and told Ag there was nothing that could be done.

"This man has swelling of the brain, a busted blood vessel in the brain, and all the blood is going to the back of his head. He is still hemorrhaging as well. There is just nothing that can be done. We'll put him in ICU and try to keep him as comfortable as possible. Past that, there is just not anything that can be done." The next morning, the nuero-surgeon confirmed their findings. That night, Artie got out of the bed, and in doing so, ripped all the wires and tubes loose that were attached to him. They had to all be re-inserted.

The days passed with no real change in his condition. Then one day, about three weeks into his stay at Oklahoma City, he could feel something happening in his head. He immediately started feeling better. When he woke up, there was an intern standing at the foot of his bed. Artie looked at him and said.

"Young man, I might have told you a lot of things over the past several days and a lot of those things you won't remember. I'm fixin to tell you something I don't want you to ever forget." He looked toward the heavens and started talking again.

"Somewhere up there is a God," he said. "And he has healed me and I'm alright. I'm going to be alright."

The intern looked at him and replied. "Yes sir," he said. "We can't do without him."

Artie knew from that moment on that the Lord had healed him. His battle was not over though. They took him in for another brain scan and it proved his brain was healed. The nuero-surgeon told him he couldn't find anything wrong with his brain and he might as well go home and go back to work. The radiologist that conducted the first brain scan couldn't believe he was healed.

"I've seen inside there and there is no way he can be healed," he said. "Let's do another scan." The next scan showed the same results. The radiologist came back and told them that Artie had normal blood flow through every blood vessel in his brain. "There is nothing wrong with him," he said. As they were wheeling him back to his room, Artie went into another coma. The blood work indicated an infection so they called in a specialist in internal medicine. It took him a few days to figure out the problem.

"His kidneys have shut down," he told Ag. "He is going to have to have prostate surgery to ever be alright." They scheduled him for surgery that very afternoon. They did the surgery on a Thursday afternoon and Artie was released the following Tuesday. It took a while for him to get to feeling well enough to get out of the house. He rode to town with his granddaughter Deanna one day and when he got back home, Carol Daube Sutton and Olive Daube (Leon Daube's wife) came to see him and brought him a box of chocolate cookies. He had eaten the hospital food for so long that he was ready for the cookies. Over the next few days and weeks, friends and neighbors would drop in to spend a little time. Nothing means more to a house bound person than visits from friends. Artie has always been blessed with a lot of friends. He has always said, "To have friends, you have to show yourself friendly."

It took a while for him to get back to where he was physically before the hospital stay. It was most evident in his driving and attention to detail that was unquestioned before the illness. One day he and Mike Pitmon had gone to Tishomingo on some errands and on the way back Artie decided to take the route through Reagan back to the ranch. He took the gravel cut-off road at the old Log Cabin Station north of Tishomingo and Mike was getting a little uneasy about the unsteady way he was handling the truck. He decided not to say anything and just ride it out. They were talking as they traveled and when Mike looked up, they were right upon the intersection with Highway #7. It was either right or left, as the road they were on ended at the intersection. Artie slammed on the brakes, but it was too late to get the truck stopped and they skidded all the way across the intersection. Luckily, the gate going into the pasture across the road was open and he skidded right through the gate and stopped in the Beck Ranch pasture. They were able to back out of the pasture and get back onto the road without any damage to the truck or the fence or anything. I think its safe to say that someone must have been watching over them that day.

To this time, Artie is quick to tell you how the Lord healed him. He's told that story all over and to a lot of people. He's told the story of his healing in various churches, sale barns, filling stations, grocery stores, and just about anywhere else folks will listen.

Top row left to right---Artie and Ag all dressed up—At the house in Mill Creek after retirement
Bottom row left to right---Artie and Ag, not sure of the location—Artie and Ag looking them over at the corrals on the West Ranch

The first real vacation Artie and Ag took was a trip to Utah. Janet was still pretty small at the time. They went with Floyd Patrick and his wife Coreen to see James Sipes who was working in Utah at the time. James worked on a seismograph crew and was in that area. They went to Salt Lake City while they were in Utah, and got the opportunity to go to the Mormon Tabernacle. Artie bought a Mormon Bible and they all toured the buildings they were allowed to go into.

While they were there, Artie spied a replica of a sea gull on a tall pole. Being naturally curious, he asked one of the guides what the pole represented. The story went like this. It seems that shortly after the Mormons settled in the area and started raising crops, crickets were eating the crops about as fast as they could plant them. They all prayed to God to save their crops and the Lord sent a flock of sea gulls to eat up all the crickets. They erected the pole with the sea gull on top of it as a memorial to the occasion. They went into the auditorium where they demonstrated the acoustics of the room by dropping a pin in the front of the building. You could hear the pin drop at the back of the building. That has stuck in Artie's mind ever since. Later, Janet and Coreen got a chance to swim in the Great Salt Lake while they were there.

Most of the time though, Artie and Ag's vacations consisted of day trips. They would take a short trip to somewhere they wanted to go or to something they wanted to see and be back in their own bed come bedtime.

PART 8: RETIREMENT 1984-20--

It all came to an end in 1984. Time to put the old cowboy out to pasture. Since 1937, he had done what he enjoyed, and that was being a cowboy. For many years now, he had been the face of Daube Ranches in the area. Along with the only girl he ever loved, it was time to relax, enjoy family and friends, and take the time to reflect on the wonderful life they have together. More time now for church and the daily prayer time that was so much a part of their lives.

THE LAST DAY

It was very early in the morning that last day on the ranch. The sun was just rising over the trees on Pennington Creek as he stood and watched the shadows disappear alongside the barn as the first rays struck them. As the walls of the saddle room came into sharp relief with the morning light, he could see the names carved into the rough boards over the years. Names of cowboys who had come and gone. None had lasted as long as he had. After all, this would be his forty seventh year on the ranch. The memories began to come as he gazed toward the east where it all began.

He could see it all so clearly as he re-lived the years in his mind. The little three room house at the feed pens as he and Ag started their life together. He could see Ag at the little wood stove as he came in from a long cold day of working in the feed lot. The wonderful smell of her biscuits baking in the oven came to him on the breeze as he stood with his boot on the bottom rail of the corral.

The Saturday nights they spent alone on the ranch when all the other cowboys had gone to town and the closeness they felt just having each other to share their hopes and dreams.

He could hear faintly the cry of his daughter as she drew her first breath in this world and he remembered how proud he was to have shared this gift of God with the only woman he ever loved.

The three of them riding across the pasture with a basket of fried chicken hanging from the saddle horn. Little Janet straining to see from her perch on the saddle behind her mother.

He could see the glow on Ag's face as the lights came on in 1949. How excited she was when they delivered the electric washing machine.

Faces of cowboys started flashing one by one in front of his eyes. They were all the men he had worked with over the years. Horses running through the tall grass caught his attention and he recognized the ones he had ridden so many miles and shared a day's work with.

He could hear the yells and shouts of the cowboys as they drove a herd of cattle toward the corral. But wait! What was that other sound that he kept hearing in the back of his mind? The sound that was so familiar, but didn't seem to go with the yells of the cowboys. As the sound became louder and more insistent, he shook his head to clear his thoughts..

"Artie!, oh Artie!." The sound finally managed to break through his daydream and as he turned toward it, he could see Ag walking down the road from the house calling his name. As she got closer, she began to speak. "What in the world were you thinking of that kept you from hearing me call?" She asked. "Breakfast has been ready for fifteen minutes."

He turned and took both her hands in his as he looked into her face. "Not a thing Dear," he said. "Not a thing." Hand in hand, they started back up the hill to the house they had shared for so many years. It was the last day of that part of their lives. It was the first day of the rest of their lives.

As they loaded up the last of their possessions from the ranch house, their lives were once again about to undergo a major change. No more cold winter days feeding the cattle. No more hot, dusty days spent vaccinating and working calves. No more endless hours patching fence and re-building water gaps. They would miss the life they lived on the ranch, they knew they would, but all things come to an end. The end of a dynasty was at hand. The ranch was changing as well though. Along with the demise of the old time cowboys, the days of the huge cow-calf operations for many ranches were coming to an end, and the Daube Ranch was no exception. As they drove away, his eyes misted as he looked once more to the east. Then he turned and looked ahead to a new life in a new place. It would be home, he knew, if Ag was there with him. He squeezed her hand gently and turned onto the highway to their new home.

Even after he retired, Artie would go and help with the roundups. Sam gave him an old gentle horse to ride that wasn't much good. Artie figured Sam thought he was just an old wore out cowboy but he thought he was still good enough to manage a good cow horse. He told Sam he wanted a good horse to ride. Sam gave him a palomino horse to ride that Everett Shaw had trained. Everett was an old time cowboy that lived up around Stonewall and did a lot of cutting horse training. Sam took the palomino up there for him to train. He made a really good cutting horse. Artie hadn't been on that palomino long before he decided he didn't need to ask for a better horse.

Artie retires after working for Daube Ranch for forty seven years

They moved into the house in Mill Creek they built for their retirement days. Close to the church where Artie would pray on a daily basis. That first year they got Glenn Anderson to plow up a garden spot and Ag put in a big garden. After that, Glenn would just come by and plow the garden without being asked. Ag loved to work in the garden and would grow much more than they could use. She would pick the vegetables and call folks on the phone to come and get what they wanted. She said she didn't mind growing and picking the vegetables, but she wasn't going to deliver them to folks. She'd call them and let them know what was available, and if they wanted them, they could come and get them. Artie always enjoyed watering the garden when it would get cooler in the late afternoon. As a kid, he loved playing in the water and that enjoyment never left him.

Sam Daube told Artie when he retired that he needed to be sure he got plenty of exercise, so he started walking five miles a day. He started walking in cowboy boots, not ever owning a pair of tennis shoes or walking shoes. Finally, Sondra Clagg asked him why he didn't get a pair of walking shoes. He said he didn't even know they made such a thing. It made all the difference in the world. He walked five miles a day for many years. Ag would walk with him at times, but she just didn't have her heart in the long walks. On one occasion, they walked out to the cemetery. They rested a while and started back. Artie offered to walk home, get the car, and come back for her, but she said she thought she could make it and she did. She didn't ever make that long of a walk again though.

Artie finally got down to three miles a day, and after he broke his foot, a mile and a half a day. He still walks that mile and a half most days, weather permitting. It's one of the things that keeps him going and active.

The retirement years were good years together for them. I know Artie especially cherishes those years, knowing their remaining time together was growing shorter. He talks fondly of the days they spent together in the house in town. The opportunities they had to look back on their life together and just be at peace.

Doak Clark was a frequent visitor and they really enjoyed his visits. Some of the time, he would stay so long that Joann would call for him to come home. After he got so he couldn't drive, he would ride his scooter to visit. Doak told Betty Clark that Artie's tomatoes were better than hers and she didn't like it. Doak figured it was due to the fertilizer Artie used. He would get fertilizer from Cooper Coles dairy at Connerville for the garden. In the later years, they had to buy fertilizer. That never did set right with Artie since he could see so much good fertilizer going to waste on all the ranches.

Top row left to right---The house Artie and Ag were living in when he retired—House east of the corrals at headquarters they lived in Bottom row left to right---Ranch House on the East ranch Artie and Ag lived in---Ranch house, I believe at the West Ranch

Church life, family, and friends filled their days. As Ag's health began to go down, they spent more time at home. Artie has been alone there now for the past ten years. He lives for his family and his church life. He loves to go to the senior citizen's dinners each week. It gives him an opportunity to visit with folks and catch up on the latest happenings. He can see a little bit out of the sides of his eyes, enough to get around and walk to church and around town. When salespeople call trying to sell him things, he tells them he is ninety-seven years old and doesn't need anything he doesn't already have. They usually tell him he doesn't sound like he is that old.

Sam Daube and Laurie Williams come by to see him on occasion. He really enjoys their visits as he does all visits. It's a good chance to reminisce about the ranch days and to ask about the ranch and what is going on. Not many of the cowboys he worked with are still living, but he loves to hear about the ones who are.

Clyde Runyan comes by to visit and they talk about the old times. Clyde's boys are about the same age as Sam Daube's boys and they would visit back and forth with each other as they were growing up. Artie said Clyde is one of the only people he knows that may have ridden more miles on a horse than he has.

Artie stays involved with the Daube Ranch as much as he can. He still goes to all the fish fries and the barbeques they have. He is an icon at the events.

Left to right---Artie, Tommie lee Jones, Jim Hook, Unidentified cowboy, Randy Putnam, Carl Runyan, Nelson Bond, Clyde Runyan, Leo Roberts, Blake Roberts, Sam Daube

He has a lot of family in the area. His daughter, Janet, and her husband Bobby live just down the road not much more than a mile from him. He has his granddaughter, Deanna and her husband, Tony Gordon, and his grandson Billye Bob close by as well. He has a great grandson Bryan Gordon, his wife Brittanie, and their daughter Bayley who is his great- great granddaughter. They live in Sulphur, Oklahoma, close enough to visit often. His other great grandson Ty Crenshaw lives at Sulphur. He is very proud of all his family and a special look comes to his face when he talks about them. He says Janet is his right arm and truly she is. Several times when I would go by to visit with him, she would be there mowing the grass or running the weed eater.

"I have had a wonderful life," he said. "Even at the age of

almost 98 years, it has been a short journey. I have turned over every rock and every stone, and I can't think of a thing that would keep me out of Heaven. I want to see all my family and friends there too."

Artie's family in 2010. Left to right- Bryan Gordon (great-grandson), Bobby Crenshaw (son-in-law), Ty Crenshaw (great-grandson), Janet Crenshaw (daughter), Artie (seated), Tony Gordon (granddaughter Deanna's husband), Deanna Gordon (granddaughter), Billye Bob Crenshaw (grandson), Bayley Gordon (great-great granddaughter in her mother's arms), Brittanie Gordon (great-grandson Bryan Gordon's wife)

POEMS & PROSE

Daddy

My daddy is a Sunday school teacher
No, he isn't a preacher
He teaches with power
That comes from studying hour after hour
It takes a lot of dedication
And a lot of meditation.
His eyes are very dim
But Jesus blesses and helps him
Jesus is always by his side
And in his heart God doth abide
In God he puts his trust
And truly his teaching blesses us.

Janet Quinton Crenshaw 7/05/1992

MOM

Momma was so very dear
For her, death held no fear
She lived a wonderful life
A good mother, grandma and wife
She lived for the day without pain
And a heavenly mansion to gain
Now her prayer would be
Please family and friends, prepare to meet me.
We Love you Aggie

Janet Quinton Crenshaw 7/25/2000

Happy Birthday Daddy

My daddy's life is so complete
He loves everyone he meets
In his little home he doth abide
But he always has Jesus by his side
He appreciates everything you do
Just do it when it's convenient for you
He is loved by old and young
Because he takes time for everyone
So Happy Birthday Daddy and my friend
On you I can always depend

Janet Quinton Crenshaw

Grandpa

You're the greatest grandpa on the earth
If you were money, there's no telling what you'd be worth
I can always count on you to pray
And I know everything will be okay
I love to hear your stories when we talk
Maybe one day we can go for a walk
When someone talks about church I think of you
God's in everything you do.
I don't see how you make it on your own
Maybe it's all those years on that strawberry roan
You walk every morning mile after mile
Oh how I love to see you laugh and smile
I know you're older but still going strong
In my eyes you can do no wrong
In our family you're the tree and I'm just the branch
Or you are the foreman just like on the ranch
You know the Bible from front to back
Just like you knew your horses and all your tack
I know when I need you I can just call
I'm so proud you are my grandpa

Billye Bob Crenshaw 11/05/2007

THE THREE FUN YEARS

The person who I admire a lot is tall and slim and has green eyes and gray hair. He is in his eighties now. Every time I visit with him he asks me about my chickens and dogs and if I'm making good grades in school. He always greets me with a great big smile and a hug. He is a very happy and cheerful man. Ever since I can remember he has always gone to church. He is a deacon in his church and always reads his Bible every day. He sets a good example, not only for me but for everyone who knows him. When I was around two years old he used to take care of me because my mom was going to school and my dad was working. He would always walk around town pulling me in a little red wagon and he gave me a hat to put on. I didn't want to wear it so I threw it on the ground. He slapped my hand gently and said "bad boy." I was always doing something to get in trouble like leaving the water on when I washed my hands and not picking up my toys. One time he got out the fly swatter and told me to pick up my toys or I was going to get a spanking. I never did that again. He taught me how to mind and respect him. When I was older I would always walk with him and he would always buy me candy and get groceries. He has so many good qualities that I can't name them all. But I will always admire my great-grandpa Artie.

Bryan Gordon
11/04/1999
6th grade

QUOTES AND COMMENTS

(Author's Note) So many people wanted an opportunity to comment on Artie and what he has meant to them. I've included this special section to accommodate as many quotes and comments as possible.

If there is such a thing as a modern day saint, that person is Artie Quinton.

Darrel Payne

I had been to Oklahoma City to see Ty and when I got home, I went by Artie's house to let him know Ty was doing some better. When I walked up to the door, I could see Artie lying on the couch and he was praying for Ty. His voice was just ringing out. It was like he was having a conversation with God. Goosebumps came up on my arms. I told Penny later, "I may have never seen an angel in my life until today, but I've seen one now."

Clyde Runyan

Artie Quinton is truly a saint of a man. I am a better Christian because of my association with him.

Doc Easley

I never saw Artie Quinton abuse a horse or a cow. You can't say that about all cowboys.

Sam Daube

Artie was the best cowman I ever saw when it came to matching cows and calves. He ran 400 head of mama cows on the East Ranch and he could tell you what calf belonged to every cow. It was uncanny how he could do that.

Sam Daube

The first time I saw Artie was approximately thirty-eight years ago when he had an aneurysm in his brain. At that time most people died with a ruptured aneurysm and of course, he did not. He lived through the ruptured aneurysm that he had. God must have had a plan for Artie that his work on this earth wasn't done. I have been taking care of him since that time. I have never seen a better person in my life. He is an extremely healthy, alert, stoic cowboy that has ridden many horses over the past many years. I also took care of his wife Agnes and many of his family. He was surrounded by excellent people. He led by example. He treated everyone with respect and was always a gentleman. It has been a pleasure knowing Artie Quinton and his family for the past 38 years.

James R. Turrentine, D.O.

There are over 300 cowboy hats representing Johnston County located inside Gene Lafitte Pharmacy. Artie Quinton's hat speaks the loudest for Johnston County history. What a legacy Artie has given to the people of this area. Not a better friend, neighbor, mentor and Christian example than Artie Quinton.

Gene Lafitte
Gene Lafitte Pharmacy
Tishomingo, Oklahoma

We have the greatest grandpa in the world. No matter what you are going through, you know he is praying for you. I have never heard him say a negative word about anyone or even say a curse word. He has stated you might have to dig a little deeper to find something good in some people, but it is always there. We were very fortunate that he and Grandma were able to keep Bryan while we worked. Lots of people call him Grandpa but always remember that I'm his favorite Granddaughter. We love you Grandpa.

Tony and Deanna (Crenshaw) Gordon

I got to stay with Artie and Aggie as a child while my mom and dad went to work. We had lots of fun and we went many a mile with my little red wagon, Artie and Aggie bought me the wagon on my 1st birthday. I actually still have my wagon and we will get to pull Bayley (our daughter) around, just like Artie pulled me. I can remember going to JT's Grocery Store and Aggie telling me I could only get one thing, and then when Grandpa and me would get there he would let me have all I wanted. I have lots of fun memories that will never go away. We love you Artie.

Love,

Bryan, Brittanie & Bayley Gordon

Great Grandson----------Great-Great Granddaughter

As a young boy, I met Artie Quinton at the Mill Creek, Oklahoma Pentecostal Holiness Church. I was about 12-13 years old. I rode horseback with him and he told me about the scriptures. As time went on and distance separated us, I never forgot what he shared with me. I later rode for Daube Cattle Co. as did he. Our meetings were on ranch work and it was as though my mentoring picked up where we left off. I knew a little more of God's wonderful word, but I loved every moment I could be where Artie was. The word of God came from his lips to me. I am a better man and minister of God's word because of Artie Quinton.

Artie Quinton, you are the best mentor and teacher a young preacher could have. Your love for God and his word instilled in me a foundation to grow and build on. Thank you my friend, mentor and Godly champion. and the greeting "Farmer, how you doing!!!"

Gale Ellis

Pentecostal Holiness Preacher

Coffeyville, Kansas

I first met Artie at the veterinary office in Sulphur in or around 1962. He was an easy man to talk to. When we took over as pastor in Mill Creek in 1964, Artie was one of three deacons in the church. He was always ready to do anything in the church that was asked of him. I never knew him to do a bad job of anything he started out to do in the church or outside the church. Artie was good to everybody and especially children. I remember when my son Keith was just about two years old he would run down the church aisle and holler. Artie gave him the nickname "Mr. Brown" because he reminded him of Walter Brown who was known for his hollering when he preached. He still calls him that to this day. Ag was a fine woman. You never had to guess where you stood with Ag. One day after church she told me, "When I go to your church, I never know if I've been to church or to a singing convention." Ag would disagree on occasion with what I had to say and we'd get into an argument over it. A day or two later, she would bring a roast or something by and say it was a peace offering.

Artie is a mild mannered man and never participated in any kind of gossip or arguing in the church. He stood up for what was right. Artie always said he wanted me to preach his funeral and I've always told him I would if I was still alive.

Artie related to people really well. He could just as easily talk to the President of the United States as he could a common man.

Frank Trent

Pentecostal Holiness Preacher
Ada Oklahoma

Artie Quinton is the same man no matter who he's talking to. There is no telling how many people he's helped over the years. You could go to him right now and get good counseling.

J.E. Quinton

Artie Quinton? Yes sir, I have to say that I consider myself quite privileged just to be able to call a man like Artie my friend. Why, his name is as synonymous with Mill Creek as is the gently flowing spring fed stream it was named after. I'm talking about a man that upon merely shaking his hand a guy can walk away with a good feeling about the encounter that he just had. Growing up around this small southern Okla. town and attending high school there allowed me the opportunity to go way back, more years than I want to admit, to when I made acquaintance with Artie. It was the early seventies when I discovered who Artie Quinton was. I said "discovered" because I believe that the good Lord just makes a way for us to once in a while happen on to some pretty grand folks in this life. Artie to me is one of those people discoveries and I realized that since the first day I met Artie and having known him down through the years, that I have been blessed with a true friend. The discovery of that friend long ago led to a friendship that remains true today. I must say that great discoveries lead to great adventures and knowing Artie Quinton has definitely been a rewarding adventure.

I always more or less associated Artie with being a kind of old west pioneer of the Mill Creek area. That impression could be for the simple reason of his being around so many years. After all one has to admit that he is a sort of ancient benchmark here. The landmark of Artie Quinton in Mill Creek, Okla. will remain permanent long after he is gone. That's just the way it is with a man of good reputation, respect, and integrity. So is Artie. But that's not all.

There has always been an atmosphere around Artie. Actually that atmosphere has always preceded him. Artie has always had the Lord's presence with him and he's always been a man of spirit. He is no doubt, probably one of the most humble men one would ever meet, a man exceedingly and abundantly glad to know his Lord and Savior Jesus Christ. He has always been ready to share the Lord with anyone who would listen. I've had the opportunity to be around Artie many times and I've found that he's always got a scripture or a word from the Lord and a desire to pray! I've always admired and respected him for that.

Well, even though Artie has grown old and his eyes have grown quite dim the vision in his heart remains vivid and has not changed. His loyalty has not changed. His gaze is toward the same place it has been fixed upon for many years, Heaven. And one day, Artie Quinton will take his journey from here to there. And if I'm still around my heart will be sad. And I will miss him greatly! But at the same time, I'll be happy for him and thankful! Thankful that I got to share with Artie and Artie got to share with me, those treasured years of friendship, on this old earth.

Jon Smith

Former Sheriff, Johnston County

Pastor: Rock Harbor Church

Ravia, Oklahoma

I'm glad Artie has lived as long as he has where I can enjoy him. He likes for me to mow his yard and when Artie and Aggie kept me he liked to watch Aggie and me play ball. I even hit rocks, his green tomatoes and his apples. He never complained. Aggie would get me if we got wild playing catch in the house. He would go watch me play football, basketball and baseball if he could see, but he encourages me. I know he is a good Christian and prays for me every day. I love my great-grandpa Artie.

Ty Crenshaw

Artie is a special person to us. Just seeing how he lives, the good job he did with his family helps others. He has shown us that no matter what, we need to keep on trying. We need God in our lives. We know he has been on some mountains and down in some valleys in his lifetime and God walked beside him all the way. He is a great teacher and a great cowboy. He is a great father, grandfather, great-grandfather, and great-great grandfather. We are so proud to call him friend. Thanks for just being there for us and anybody else who has a need or wants a friend.

Bob & Patsy Hook

To my brother Artie Quinton

We share the same daddy. We are half brother and sister. His grandparents on his mother's side reared him to a young lad. I was an infant when he came to live with us so my earliest memories to me he was grown. Oh the joy of knowing him as I grew up. He always has a smile for everyone and something good to say about everyone. He never met a person he didn't find quality in. He always says "he or she is a good person." He has always been my hero. A finer Christian you will never meet. I thought he could set on a horse with more pride and joy than any cowboy I knew. To me he was a real cowboy. I loved his hat, boots and he always wore long sleeves and that made him look dressed to go anywhere. He loved his animals but most of all he loved his Ag. He was a wonderful loving husband. So was his Aggie as we later called her, a wonderful wife. They were loving parents to Janet. They were blessed with 2 grandchildren, 2 great grandchildren and a great-great granddaughter. He retired when he was 72 and he and Ag moved to town and he started walking for exercise. I later joined him. He kept it up and I should have. Artie is legally blind so when he is out walking and he doesn't recognize your voice, tell him who you are. He will be 98 in Oct. That may seem like a lot of years but God's word teaches us we are but a vapor, here today and gone tomorrow. We have both out lived our mates but we both have faith, hope and joy in the morrow we'll be reunited.

Ted has written a couple of books already and they are

good reading. We look forward to reading this one. Many thanks to Ted. Life is short even if you lived to be 100. To my loving brother and my hero.

Your loving sister,

Betty Clark

My first church was Mill Creek Baptist Church. I was a student at the seminary in Fort Worth, TX and drove to Mill Creek on the weekends. Because of the distance, we were not able to have Wednesday night services; so, our people went to other churches for midweek services. Being a "good" Baptist, I was uneasy about that arrangement until I met Artie, who belonged to the church most of our people were attending. He impressed me as one of the deepest spiritual men I had ever met. I discovered that the name on the church was not as important as the quality of the people who belonged there. From then on, I was at peace with our people being around folks like Artie.

Over the years, I have seen Artie in a variety of situations. He has shown up at funerals to encourage folks in sorrow. He has attended community and ranch gatherings to demonstrate his interest in the lives of the people in the Mill Creek area. Even as his eyesight deteriorated, he has maintained an inspiring connection with his church, friends, and community. He became very adept at recognizing voices and still lights up when he hears you speak to him. In every circumstance, he has maintained a gracious spirit and an attitude of Christian hospitality.

In the Bible, the writer of Hebrews speaks of a "cloud of

witnesses" whose testimonies inspire the believer to persevere and overcome. Artie Quinton's testimony of commitment to family values, dedication and service to his church, love for his community and others, perseverance through the challenges that have come in his life, and his faith that stood out in everything he did has made him part of the cloud of witnesses that continues to challenge and inspire my life. I have a "short list" of people that I feel provide the closest picture of the Biblical admonition to imitate Christ; Artie Quinton is most assuredly on that list. I am proud, blessed and humbled to be able to call Artie Quinton my friend.

Brother Eddie Malphrus

Artie Quinton is truly a legend in our community. I believe he is the only one true constant in our lives. To me, Artie is Moses, Noah, David, Job, and Elisha all rolled into one. He is the one individual that all men wish they could be. I believe that everyone in the southern part of the United States either knows him or has heard of him. As for me, I have had the honor of knowing Artie, (I call him Dad), all my life. I can truthfully say that his Christian teachings have saved my life more than once. To me, the name "Artie Quinton" is synonymous with "Lord", "Jesus", "Father", and "Dad". I can't think of Artie without thinking of the Lord Jesus. Artie first came into my life as a Sunday school teacher and taught me the way of the Lord at an early age. I can still remember his caring ways and patience with some of my "not so correct ways" of behaving and some of my answers to his biblical questions. At times, he would chuckle at my enthusiastic answers and then, ever so slightly, correct my answer in a way that still made me feel good and correct at the same time.

He has been my mainstay and an example of how I should live my life. He has been the leading Christian example as a father, husband, brother, and leader in the community. He has never turned down a person in need and when asked for advice, he always prefaces his statement with a smile and "You know if the Lord".

Just to be around Artie is a blessing. I love sitting beside him in church and hearing him talk. You see, Dad is what I would call a living Bible and to hear him recite scripture is to feel as if the Lord were sitting beside you and saying it himself. To hear him pray is like listening to poetry. When we go to the alter, I always rush to be near him so I can hear him pray. He is always so humble in prayer and his prayers are so eloquent they sound like poetry or the heavenly choir itself. On occasion, I believe the Holy Spirit touches him and he will suddenly give a small jerk and begin to laugh in the spirit. At that moment, the power of the Holy Spirit envelopes everyone around him. I hope that by listening to him pray, I will someday be able to pray in the same manner.

I can say that I have been one blessed man to have had Artie in my life. Because he has let God lead his way and use him, he has changed countless lives, mine included. I want to say a very humble thank you to Artie for being there for me. May our Lord God bless you forever.

Love you Dad
Brian Tolbert

I thank God for blessing me with a friend like Artie. He is the kindest, sweetest, faithful, Christian I know. I admire Artie for having one wife, one job, and one church.

Love you Artie

Kelly Conner

I married Artie's half-sister Ruby, but instead of a brother-in-law, I think of him as a brother. Ruby loved Artie as much as she loved her other family. He is as strong a Christian as you will find. He has touched more lives than he will ever know. It is a blessing to be around him. I love him very much. If I needed him in the wee hours of the night, he would be there for me.

Harmon Clark

Brother-in-law

We first met Artie in 1976 when we came to pastor the Mill Creek Church where he has always attended. He was such a dedicated Christian man in every way. He served as deacon and Sunday school teacher and was so faithful in his service to the church and to God. He continued teaching for many years though he was slowly losing his sight. He has been a joy to work with and a dear friend whom we love.

Jerry and Linda George

When I was down flat on my back, Artie Quinton and Arvel Pitmon came to my house every day and most of the time they walked when no one could bring them. They were faithful in the snow and bad weather. Artie is still a blessing to me and is at church whenever the doors are open. He says "A lot of people are just fair weather Christians." He is an example for all of us.

Travis Vaughan
Mill Creek Oklahoma

I have known Artie at least 70 years. He is one of the strongest friends I've had in my life. He has the best memory of anyone I ever knew. He knows more about my family than I know. I know he prays for me every day. If you are around him for five minutes, he is talking about the Lord and prays a beautiful prayer directly from his heart. He is a true friend.

A.D. "Denzil" Jordan
Mill Creek Oklahoma

I don't remember ever not knowing Artie. He has told me many times he knew me before I was born. I believe that. I've always been in awe of him. A man with Hollywood looks, and an aura of an angel or a saint. The bible says, "no man goes without sin." Somehow, I can't believe that of Artie. I've had tremendous respect and love for him. I mostly saw him at his dad's or at church. I can still see him standing in prayer with tears streaming down his face. I felt he had a direct line to Heaven. He always counted the congregation at church because he could do it so fast. It was like he was on horseback counting cattle out on the ranch. Our family was most appreciative that he honored our mother's wishes and preached her funeral. She was always afraid he would go first and wouldn't be there for her but he was, and he did a great job. So it is with these memories and so many more that I always wish Artie a Happy Birthday on Oct. 30th.

Thanks for the example.

Respectfully,

Aileen Holder

Brother Artie is one of the finest people I have ever known. He really "practices what he preaches." He never fails to offer me a smile, kind words, and encouragement. I feel blessed to have him praying for me and my family. I just love him to pieces!

Darlene Pittman

It is a great honor for me to say a few words about Artie Quinton. Over the years I have given a lot of thought as to why I have so much love, respect, and admiration for Artie. My conclusion is that Artie exemplifies each of the fruits of the spirit (love, joy, peace, patience, kindness, goodness, faithfulness, gentleness, self-control) in a more complete way than anyone else I know. When you add humility to these 9 characteristics you have a "Man after God's own heart". When I am in his presence I feel the love of Jesus shining through him. The world would say he didn't accomplish much. He never made a lot of money, never lived in a fancy house; he didn't drive a luxury car. His life shows us that we do not need the things the world offers to live victoriously. I cannot imagine anyone having any more rewards in Heaven that Artie.

Larry Hobbs

When my daughter Cherity was a baby she had a really bad fever one night. Her fever was over 105 degrees. I called the doctor and he said to get her into a tub of cold water and put rubbing alcohol on her. We were not able to take her to the hospital because the roads were covered with sleet and snow. I remember Mother and Daddy saying we needed to pray. I immediately asked Daddy to call Artie. Daddy was on the phone with Artie and they were both praying and you could just tell God was listening to every word. Within minutes, Cherity's fever was back to normal and she was feeling much better. If you do not have a personal relationship with our savior, you are missing out on the life God meant for us to live. Artie Quinton walks with God every second of every day and I am so blessed to know him. Thank you Artie and my family for your blessed prayers. Your faith and God's power made it possible for my little girl to be on the road to recovery that very second.

Love you lots and lots Artie

Cheryl Parker

Artie is my direct link to my papa Elmore Garrison who passed away in 1987. I love Artie with all my heart and he has always called me his "Little Red." I'm always uplifted when I see Artie. He is such a strong person and Christian warrior, that I can only hope and pray to have half the faith he does. Artie always has a story to tell me about my papa and the things they got into while growing up. I love Artie and feel extremely blessed to know him. He is such a remarkable man.

Jamie Vestal

Artie is the wisest man I have ever met. I am absolutely in awe of how he can remember everything. I consider him my spiritual father. He has been such an encouragement to me. There have been many times when I felt I just couldn't go on anymore and he would lift me up with his encouraging words. I don't mean to be morbid, but I often think of what I am going to do when Artie goes home to be with the Lord, I know he prays for me every day, and I am going to miss that. I've never met anyone like him, and I love him very much.

Sharon Beratto

I have known Artie all my life. Rather, I should say that Artie has known me all my life. That is just who Artie is. A short conversation with Artie will soon reveal that he knows your family. Artie has this ability to remember people – not just their name but who they are kin to. And that is because he is sincerely interested in you. I have counted it an honor to be able to pastor the church Artie attends. I don't know if I could really say that I am his pastor because he teaches and leads me more than I could ever him. Over the past six years that I have been pastor at Mill Creek, I don't recall one Sunday service going by that Artie did not say something positive about the service. If for some reason we did not get to greet each other after the morning service, Artie would greet me that evening saying, "I didn't get to tell you this morning but I believe what you preached." Artie has inspired many people throughout the years with his teaching, his willingness to work, and his knowledge of the word of God. But most of all Artie has lived out the 13th chapter of First Corinthians that says, "Though I speak with the tongues of men and of angels, and have not charity, I am become as sounding brass, or a tinkling cymbal. And though I have the gift of prophecy, and understand all mysteries, and all knowledge; and though I have all faith, so that I could remove mountains, and have not charity, I am nothing." It is the love that Artie has for people that has made him one of the greatest men I have ever known and one of the greatest men the Mill Creek community and churches have ever known. If the Mill Creek Pentecostal Holiness Church, the Mill Creek community or I learn anything from Artie's life, I would hope that it would be to have love for one another and that includes our enemies.

Darryl Patrick
Pastor, Mill Creek Pentecostal Holiness Church

MEMORIES OF MY MOM AND DAD

Some of my earliest remembrances are centered on life as a family. We did things together as a family. We would ride pasture, sometimes stopping to swim or fish. We gathered a lot of pecans together. I knew I was growing up in a Christian family and I always knew my mother and daddy were praying for me. Momma always had prayer with me before I went to school every morning.

I believe if there was ever a marriage made in Heaven, their marriage was. The first time they saw each other, they knew they were meant for each other. They always got along well and compromised when they didn't agree.

Mother always wanted to be a school teacher but never got the chance. She would help me with my homework and we would get into a fuss fight. We would get the same answer to a math problem, but would get to it in a different way. We would argue until my dad would finally step in and tell us to put the homework away for a little while.

One time my momma called me "wishy washy" and I cried and cried because I thought she called me a bad name. I couldn't wait 'til my daddy got home so I could tell on her for saying it. When I told him what she said, he laughed and laughed.

We would go to all the revivals. That was back when revivals lasted as long as two whole weeks. We would go every night. One night we were coming home from a revival and the snow was so deep they had to walk the last mile to the house. Daddy wrapped me in a blanket and carried me home.

One night when we got home from church Daddy put the car in the garage. Momma stepped out and a water moccasin wrapped around her ankle and bit her. I remember being so afraid she would die. I had always heard if you got bit by a snake you would die. She had to stay the night in the Delay Hospital at Sulphur.

I remember Daddy going to the Daube Department Store on Saturday to do business and Momma and I would walk downtown to the Drug Store. We would always have a BLT, chips, and a coke. I always enjoyed that so much.

My mother was an excellent cook. She didn't like for me to be in the kitchen too much. I was left handed and she always said it looked like I was just about to stir whatever I was stirring clean out of the bowl. We always had company on Sunday and the company would stay and visit. There was always time to visit back then.

Daddy is the most thankful and thoughtful person I know. If he asks for something he always says "at your convenience."

After Mother died, I remember him saying he didn't ever want to hear me say I missed going somewhere or doing something because of him. He is legally blind, can't watch television or read his Bible. He can't drive, so is dependent on me or someone to take him places he needs to go. He can't call people on the phone except for the few numbers that are programmed into his phone. There are raised dots on the numbers he can feel.

Despite these encumbrances, he is quick to tell folks how blessed he is. I am truly blessed to have had such wonderful, loving, and caring parents.

Janet Quinton Crenshaw

Artie and Clyde Runyan at the West Ranch Corrals

HISTORICAL REFERENCE

Bellwood and Mill Creek area birth record year 1912.

Still living

Artie Otto Quinton
Altha Smithers Attebery

Deceased

Willie Lee (Brock) Ross

Woodrow Cobb

Vic Willis

Carl Drake

Norris Lester

Acie Fox

Leroy Tignor

Lena Stewart

Leon Seeley

Herschel Brewer

Willie Beavers

Mabel Montague

Jewel Rowe

Earl Tisdell

Frank Halley

Billie Reddy

Granny Samis

George Jordan

Elsie Johnson

Joe Garrison

Arvel Slaughter

Pearline Trammel

Thelma Austin

Willie (Duter) Conner

A PARTIAL LISTING OF DAUBE RANCH EMPLOYEES DURING ARTIE'S WORKING YEARS, 1937 TO 1984.

Bus Goodson

Odell Webb

Bunt Tisdell

Paul Mills

Darrell Cothran

Jim Crenshaw

David Cook

Jude kingsberry

Glenn Trammel

Finis Clement

Ab Howard

Jim Hook

Bobby Crenshaw

Mike Pitmon

Herschel Brewer

Walt Miller

John Ed (Doc) Spears

Doyle Pittman

Elmore Garrison

Richard Pitmon

Leroy Pitmon

JB Johnston

Don Payne

Gale Ellis

Tom Cardwell

Leo Roberts

Various young men who stayed and worked on the ranch on a temporary basis.

During the feed pen days, other employees included.

Chester Belcher
Raymond Howard
Paul Burk
Mooch Parker
Duter Conner
Red Akins
Bill Belcher

A HISTORY OF THE MILL CREEK PENTECOSTAL HOLINESS CHURCH

Although most of the original members came from the Bellwood Church, the Mill Creek Holiness Church got its start in the very early 1940's when a Lady named Mrs. W. P. Harris from Kingston, Oklahoma came to Mill Creek and said she had a vision for the church. She called the vision "Let's go back to Bethel." She held church in several buildings on Main Street for a while, then she went back to Kingston.

Nadine McKinney deeded land to the church, and in 1942 a new church building was built on that land. The church is still there at the time of this writing. Oscar Moore was Conference Superintendent at the time and he brought 10 preachers down with him and they framed up a 24 foot by 40 foot building in one day. That was the first real Holiness Church in Mill Creek.

The first pastor in the new church was Clayton Morgan. He paid his own house rent which was $20 a month. Eva Garrison was pastor from 1948 until 1953. They called her "Weva." She said she never really wanted to preach and the Lord had to constantly whip her to get her behind the pulpit. She said she wasn't called to preach, she was called to go out into the highways and hedges and work for the Lord. She was really good at doing that very thing. She and Florence Patrick were really close. They always told each other that when one of them died, the other one would pray for their family regularly. George and Florence Patrick had twelve children. George would bring Florence by the Holiness Church and drop her off, then he would go to church at the Baptist Church. When Church was over, he'd come back by and pick her up. That might qualify him as the first real "go getter."

K.R. Jones took over the pastoral duties from Eva Garrison in 1954 and stayed through the next year. He built a parsonage in 1955 and the cost was a little over $700. Of course all the labor was furnished by the men of the church and the men from the Baptist Church came over and helped shingle the roof.

When Brother Jones left, Eva Garrison pastored again for a very short time. Donald Burchett took over in 1956. He would stay and pastor until 1962. He was just a young "Whipper Snapper" at the time and he loved to hunt and fish. It wasn't uncommon to see him and the Payne boys tramping across the field hunting Jack rabbits. He also loved to fish and he gigged a lot of suckers on Mill Creek in the wintertime. You could hear him laughing from a mile away. Artie gave Donald's oldest son the nickname "Grasshopper."

Ed Harris pastored from 1962 until 1964 when Frank Trent took over the church. Frank added 10 foot to the building and put in the first bathrooms for the church. The sewer system was installed in Mill Creek in 1962 as well. Brother Trent stayed at the church until 1972 then moved to Ada to Pastor the church there. He would preach at that church for almost forty years. If he is able, Frank is going to preach Artie's funeral and sing some songs as well.

Richard McAnally took over the church from Brother Trent and preached a couple of years. After Brother McAnally, there were Charles Harleson, Tommy Tomlison, Melvin Garrison, Jerry George, and Butch Fires. Melvin started the new church and Butch Fires did a lot of finish work. Butch, Artie, and Elmore Garrison, did most of the work on the fellowship hall. Ag thought a lot of Butch Fires and he felt the same way about her. They had the kind of relationship where they felt like they could say about anything to each other and the other one would understand.

One particular Sunday, Brother Butch felt like he had preached an above average sermon and was really feeling good about it. After the services, as he stood at the door and shook hands with the congregation Ag came by and hit him with her cane as she went by. ***"That's the worst sermon I ever heard,"*** she said. She loved him though and when she passed away July 25th 2000; he conducted her funeral at her request. Later on, Jerry George pastored again. Darryl Patrick followed Brother George and still pastors there today.

As a kid growing up in Mill Creek in the 1950s, I was just

a little bit afraid to go by the Holiness Church when they were having services, especially at night. I had grown up in the rather sedate Methodist Church and some of the wailing and shouting that would sometimes pour out of the Holiness Church was just a little more than a kid that didn't grow up with it could handle. I remember David Roberson and I would dare each other to ride by on a bicycle at night when services were going on. I don't know if we were afraid the Lord would grab us as we rode by or if some of the devils they were casting out would jump on us. I remember one summer night in 1957, David and I were sitting on our bicycles a block north of the church trying to get up the nerve to ride down the street past the church. We argued back and forth about which one of us was going to do it, and finally David allowed as how it was his turn so he would do it.

I circled a block west and turned south at the hardware store while David headed down the street in front of the church. Just before he got even with the church, he could see someone, a woman, running up the church aisle toward the front door of the church. She was shouting and had her arms held up high in the air above her head as she ran. David was sure she had seen him and was after him. He tried to make a bat-turn to go back north, but his bicycle slid in the loose gravel and down he went in the middle of the street. He got that bicycle back up on its wheels as fast as he could and headed south down the street to our rendezvous point by the school house. I could see him coming in the half-light almost a block away. He was skinned down both arms, and the knees were out of his jeans as well. The frayed denim around his knees was fast becoming red as the blood flowed freely down his legs. We hurried as fast as we could to his house where his mom cleaned him up and doctored his wounds. That about ended our little relationship with the Holiness Church. My family has attended that very same church for well over thirty years now. I wonder if I will ever hear the shouting again and see folks running up and down the aisles. If I do, I hope there is a young boy on a bicycle there to see it and wonder like I did over fifty years ago.

INTERESTING FACTS AND PRETTY GOOD GUESSES

- *Artie has lived within a 10 mile radius of where he was born his entire life.*

- *The Bellwood area got its name in the middle 1800s from a woman who was a girlfriend of a man named Quinton. Her name was Belle, and it is thought that her last name was either Wood or Woods. (Story #1 and my favorite)*

- *But then, Bellwood might have gotten its name from a hollow tree, that when struck with a stout branch, would give off a sound with a bell-like quality. It supposedly stood in the area where the well that was called "the public well" stood. (Story #2 is from a pretty good source) By the way, the source asked me not to use his name.*

- *There was one more theory about the source of the Bellwood name that I uncovered during my many visits with folks around the area. The story goes like this. There was a Frenchman living in the area in or around 1850. He had a shack built in close proximity to a grove of trees. The French term "belle", is often used for an attractive wooded area. The Frenchman, when asked where he lived, would always give his location as the house by the Bellewood. The name was somehow shortened to "Bellwood" over the years. I would be interested in hearing from others who know, or think they know, where the name originated. Now I'm really curious.*

- *It takes more muscles to frown then it does to smile. (One of Artie's favorite sayings)*

- *There were three houses on the Kemp Estate in the 1920s and folks living in all three houses carried water from the same well over a quarter of a mile. None of the three families chose to locate their house in close proximity to the well. (What am I missing here?)*

- *There was a Post Office at the small settlement of Al Hambra until the year 1900. It was just west of Pennington Creek about three quarters of a mile west and north of Horace Cook's present home.*

- *The bridge commonly referred to as "The Bray Bridge" was called "The Red Bridge" for a long period of time due to the red paint applied to the metal bridge when it was built. The bridge was once about thirty feet longer than it is today.*

- *The Daube Ranch brand as seen on the horse on the cover of this book is "Double O Bar." As a kid growing up surrounded by Daube Ranches, the brand was most often referred to as the "Double Dot" It's hard for me to get used to the "Double O Bar" enunciation after so many years of hearing it called the "Double Dot"*

- *You can stand at the corrals on Daube's West Ranch and see into what were three school districts in the 1930's. Frisco, Bellwood, and Mill Creek. They all cornered just south of the corrals. There were three houses on the West Ranch, none of them over a quarter of a mile from the corrals, and each was in a different school district.*

Artie Quinton 2004.

Artie at the West Ranch Corrals in 2010

Artie relaxing on the corral fence at the West Ranch

Artie and Clyde Runyan talk it over

Artie in the saddle house door at the West Ranch

Artie rode this saddle for several years just before he retired. It was hand-made at Randolph Saddle Shop in Ardmore, Oklahoma and presented to him by Sam Daube.

THE LAST WORD

The old man walked slowly along, pushing the walker ahead of him as he went. He needed it now-a-days to keep his balance as he made his daily mile and a half walk around the gravel streets of Mill Creek, Oklahoma. The wind was cold and he drew his jacket closer about his neck as he turned up Delaware Street into the north wind. He struggled into the wind, the tennis shoes making a crunching sound in the gravel with each step. A draft of cold air found its way into the blue coveralls he habitually wore and he shivered in spite of himself. In some ways, this mile and a half walk was just as hard as the walk to school was in 1918. Some ninety-two years had passed since then and it seems life is still a struggle. He squinted his eyes to try to see the road ahead. It was hard to see anything these days. The doctor said he was legally blind and had been for some time. As he continued on, his thoughts drifted back to the time when Ag was still with him. She's been gone over 10 years now, but her memory is still as fresh as it was the day they laid her to rest. A smile momentarily crossed his lips as he thought of the first time they met while walking to church. In his mind's eye, he could see the little house at the feed pens they shared in 1937 as they began their life together. The air was getting colder, it had the feel of snow in it. As he looked ahead, he thought he could see the footbridge over Polecat Creek. Not much further to go. As he raised his head and looked toward the heavens, the smile came back to his face. No, not much further to go. Not much further at all.

EPILOGUE

The story of the life of Artie Quinton is a study in how a man is shaped by life and God to become the person he is today. He is the epitome of what is good and right in this carnal world and living proof of how a person can overcome obstacles in life to become a benchmark for what we all want to be. Artie is truly a special person who has had a positive influence in my life and the lives of countless others. He is the kind of man that, just being around him makes you want to be a better person. God has healed him from an illness that was certain to end his life, and He did it because He had more work for Artie to do. I know this in my heart.

As I've researched this book, I've learned a lot about the country around Mill Creek and how it was in the early years of the 20th century. How the residents of this area lived, how they thought, and what was important to them. These people were the salt of the earth. They are what made this country. They worked hard, played hard, and lived life with an intensity you cannot find today. It was not an easy life, but it bred a generation of Americans that are a dying breed. Whatever happened to the patriotism and faith in God that so defined folks of that era?

I've also learned a lot about Artie Quinton. How his faith in God is perpetuated in his daily life. How deep his feelings are for his family and for people in general. How he always has a positive outlook on life regardless of the circumstances of the moment. How he loves chicken strips with mashed potatoes and gravy. How his entire face lights up when he smiles.

The most important thing in Artie's life is his relationship with God. He will very quickly tell you that without you having to ask. He said the Lord told him to pray at least an hour every day and he does that very thing, often putting in some overtime to boot. He has told me several times that God allowed him to spend the last few years of his life living close to the church because he knew he would be blind and would have trouble getting to church to pray.

I've learned things about myself as well while spending time with Artie and traveling around the country gathering data and material for this book. I didn't have as rough of a time growing up as I thought I did compared to the trials of living in the early part of the 20th century. I realize even more how good God has been to me and my family over the years and how much closer to Him I've grown just listening to Artie's ministry. We would end each of our sessions together with prayer and the presence of God was so strong as Artie prayed that I almost felt as if I would see Him standing there with us when I looked up.

I want to again thank all the people who spent time with me as I worked on this writing. Thanks for sharing your stories and thoughts so generously. I've laughed and I've cried as I've written down the memories people have of this astounding man. I've never heard him say a bad word about any person. I will cherish the hours I spent with him as we talked about his life and life in general. Artie is a truly unique man.

One afternoon as we were talking, I asked Artie how he would like for folks to remember him. He thought for a few seconds. "I'd like to be remembered as a caring person," He said. "I'd crawl on my knees and ask forgiveness from anyone I've hurt during my life. I believe to live right, you've got to have a forgiving heart and a repentant spirit."

Artie likes to visit with folks and share his thoughts. He has a wealth of knowledge about the Bible and a deep conviction of how he believes God wants him to live. Go by and visit with him. He'll welcome you into his home and will really enjoy your company. You'll leave there with your spirit renewed and a better outlook on life. I guarantee it! Thank you Artie, for sharing your memories with me.

Ted L. Pittman

ABOUT THE AUTHOR

Ted Pittman has written about the evolution of the southern and central areas of Oklahoma in short story form and in historical fiction. "Bellwood Cowboy" is his first venture into the arena of biographical writing. Ted was raised in the area that is the setting of this book and has hunted and fished over all the area that is home to the characters in Bellwood Cowboy.

Ted started writing after friends suggested he put the stories of his childhood in print. That started a love for writing that has led to the publication of "Black Cotton," a collection of short stories from the 1950s era, and "Son Of The Red Earth," a historical fiction set in the Great Depression days of the 1930s. "Bellwood Cowboy" chronicles the life of Artie Quinton, a life-long cowboy who is truly one of a dying breed. He is the last of the old time cowboys. There are currently thousands of Ted's books in circulation.

Ted and his wife Darlene reside in Sulphur, Oklahoma. They have four children and eleven grandchildren. His interests, outside of writing, include boating and fishing, walking in the park, outdoor cooking, and spending time with family. Ted is a business manager for a major corporation and has worked for the same company for almost forty years.

TRY THESE OTHER BOOKS BY TED L. PITTMAN

"Black Cotton" is a collection of short stories that depict actual events in the life of the author in the era of the 1950s and early 1960s. Writing under the pen name "Peter Lynn', the author re-lives the adventures of a young boy growing up in rural Oklahoma before the time of microwave ovens, color television, and computers. A time when people felt safe to leave their doors unlocked and had time to visit with neighbors on a slow summer afternoon.

Below is a short excerpt from one of the stories in "Black Cotton". In this story, young Petey and a friend decide to hop a freight train down to the "ole swimming hole". Like many plans are apt to do, it doesn't work out quite like they had intended.

I began to worry a little when we were just a mile from the Rock Wool Plant and the train wasn't slowing down. Not to worry, they probably stop pretty sudden like anyway. When we passed the Rock Wool Plant doing about 50 miles per hour, I knew we'd had it. What happened? Train stopped here every day. Seen 'em do it a thousand times. Glory Be! What now? Davey's face was a little green when I sneaked a look in his direction. I knew it! I knew it! He kept saying. You've done it again. I won't be able to sit down for a month when my daddy gets through walloping me. Oh Lordy! Where we going? How we gonna get home? Won't ever get home! Oh Lordy. Won't ever see Momma again. What we gonna eat? Shut up, I says. This train gotta stop somewhere ain't it? When it stops, we get off and walk home. That's all there is to it.

"Son Of The Red Earth" is a historical fiction set in the central and southern parts of Oklahoma during the depression years of the early 1930s. Based on a true story, the book depicts the life of young Jorney Wilson as he strives to live with an abusive and alcoholic father. Sold off to a neighboring farmer for the sum of $50 he vows to not take another beating. He finds he has to fight to keep that very thing from happening. With Silas Baldwin down on the ground and maybe dead, he turns to a life of running and hiding from the law. He finds the girl of his dreams and some lasting friendships along the way. Caught with a truck load of moonshine whisky, he finds himself on trial in Atoka County for a murder he didn't commit. Follow his life and trial as he fights to be free as a

"Son Of The Red earth." The following is an excerpt from the book.

It was a Friday in late October 1934. I was looking forward to seeing Betsy the next night at the movie house. Shortly after the noon break, we were headed back to the Pavillion Springs area to put the finishing touches on the open air building we had constructed over the springs. I was taking the crew down to the springs while Bulldog was finishing up a little paper work at the camp. He was gonna meet us at the springs after he finished up. Bulldog really struggled with the paperwork, and I wasn't much better. At least he had a high school diploma. What little schooling I had gotten didn't go far when it came to figuring and such. The paperwork had to be done though. Without the paperwork being turned in every month, nobody was gonna get paid, and not getting paid was not a very popular thing around the C.C.C. camp. I was glad Bulldog volunteered to do it this month. Figuring up the payroll and getting it turned in was sure to give me a headache every time.

We hadn't much more than gotten back down to the springs when here came Bulldog down the trail flogging his old mule for all he was worth. Bulldog had taken to riding a mule around the park the last few weeks. Said his lumbago was bothering him too much to have to walk all over the park. That old mule was really working up a lather the way Bulldog was pushing him down the trail. He slid off the mule just as he got to where I was standing. He grabbed me by the shirt and half dragged me behind a bunch of cedars growing alongside the trail.

"You men get on back to work," he hollered! "This ain't no concern of yours."

He whirled around and grabbed me by the shirt right up close to the collar and dragged my face down close to his.

"Is Billy Bates your real name? Don't lie to me boy! Tell me the truth! Is Billy Bates your real name?"

Before I could answer, he started talking again.

"Cause if your name might happen to be Jorney Wilson, there are two Federal Marshals back at camp looking to take you in. That you boy? Your name Jorney Wilson?"

I just nodded. I was dumbstruck. Couldn't talk. Old Bulldog was doing all the talking anyhow, so I just stood there and listened.

"Boy, you head off down the creek 'til you get into the thick woods past the Rock Creek Campground. Wait 'til it gets dark, then ease up to town. The white house right behind the old lodge building! You know where it is. That's Millie Rogers' house. Tell her Bulldog said to feed you and keep you hid 'til I get there. Now go! Get out of here before them Federal boys take a notion to come down here looking for you."

I started to open my mouth to say something, but he just shoved me toward the trail to Rock Creek Campground.

"Just shut up and go. Remember, go to Millie's house after dark. I'll meet you there."

LaVergne, TN USA
02 March 2011
218325LV00004B/2/P

9 781452 096803